The Consolation of Nature

The Consolation of Nature

Spring in the Time of Coronavirus

MICHAEL McCARTHY

JEREMY MYNOTT

PETER MARREN

HODDERstudio

First published in Great Britain in 2020 by Hodder Studio
An Hachette UK company

2

Copyright © Michael McCarthy, Jeremy Mynott and Peter Marren 2020

The rights of Michael McCarthy, Jeremy Mynott and Peter Marren
to be identified as the Authors of the Work has been asserted by them
in accordance with the Copyright, Designs and Patents Act 1988.

Maps by Rodney Paull
Map sketch by Hannah Smith

Quotation on p.46 used with permission from the
Philip Larkin Estate and Faber and Faber Ltd.

A CIP catalogue record for this title is available from the British Library

Hardback ISBN 9781529349153
eBook ISBN 9781529349160

Typeset by Palimpsest Book Production Ltd, Falkirk, Stirlingshire

Printed and bound in Great Britain by Clays Ltd, Elcograf S.p.A.

Hodder & Stoughton policy is to use papers that are natural, renewable
and recyclable products and made from wood grown in sustainable forests.
The logging and manufacturing processes are expected to conform to
the environmental regulations of the country of origin.

Hodder & Stoughton Ltd
Carmelite House
50 Victoria Embankment
London EC4Y 0DZ

www.hodder-studio.com

Contents

For
Caroline Lucas
from
all three of us

Michael McCarthy

Michael McCarthy is one of Britain's leading writers on the environment and the natural world. As a journalist, he was the Environment Correspondent of *The Times*, covering the early measures taken to combat climate change, culminating in the Earth Summit at Rio de Janeiro; later he was the long-standing Environment Editor of the *Independent*. He has won a string of awards for his work, including Environment Journalist Of The Year in the British Environment and Media Awards (three times); Specialist Writer of the Year in the British Press Awards; the Silver Medal of the Zoological Society of London; the Dilys Breeze Medal of the British Trust for Ornithology; and the Medal of the RSPB for 'outstanding services to conservation'. As an author he has written *Say Goodbye to the Cuckoo* (2009), a study of Britain's summer migrant birds, which was widely praised; and *The Moth Snowstorm: Nature and Joy* (2015), which was shortlisted for the Wainwright Prize and the Richard Jefferies Prize. *The Moth Snowstorm* was described by the *New York Times* as 'an idiosyncratic and wonderful walk through his joy of nature'.

Michael's patch, in normal times, is the Royal Botanic Gardens, Kew, in south-west London, and in particular Kew's bluebell wood, an enchanting wild survival in the capital city. When Kew Gardens closed for the lockdown however, it became the nearby towpath of the River Thames, especially the section between Richmond Bridge and Kew Bridge, which is tidal; Richmond Park, the historic, 2,400-acre landscape of acid grassland, streams and ancient oak woods, largely unchanged since Charles I enclosed it in 1637, which is the largest of the royal parks and remarkably wildlife-rich; and the leafy suburban streets on the borders of Richmond and Kew, which themselves benefit from the proximity of such a large amount of green space.

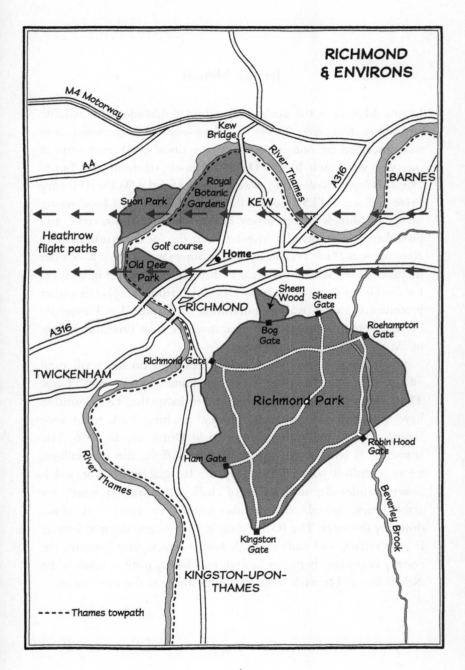

RICHMOND & ENVIRONS

M4 Motorway

Kew Bridge

River Thames

A4

A316

BARNES

Royal Botanic Gardens

Syon Park

KEW

Heathrow flight paths

Golf course

Home

Old Deer Park

Sheen Wood

Sheen Gate

RICHMOND

Bog Gate

Roehampton Gate

A316

Richmond Gate

TWICKENHAM

Richmond Park

River Thames

Robin Hood Gate

Ham Gate

Beverley Brook

Kingston Gate

KINGSTON-UPON-THAMES

----- Thames towpath

Jeremy Mynott

Jeremy Mynott is the author of various publications on wildlife and nature. *Birdscapes: Birds in Our Experience and Imagination* (2009) was described by one reviewer as 'the finest book ever written on why we watch birds'. His latest book, *Birds in the Ancient World: Winged Words* (2018), was shortlisted for the Wolfson History Prize and was a TLS Book of the Year. He also led a biodiversity survey of Shingle Street, a tiny hamlet on the Suffolk coast, and published the results as a love-letter to the local environment in *Knowing your Place: Wildlife in Shingle Street* (2016). He is a founder member of 'New Networks for Nature' and co-author of a report for the Green Party on A New Deal for Nature (2019). His earlier professional career was in publishing at Cambridge University Press, where he became chief executive. He is an Emeritus Fellow of Wolfson College, Cambridge.

Jeremy's patch is in West Suffolk, centered on the small rural village of Little Thurlow, which is joined to its twin, Great Thurlow, by a road, a river and a web of footpaths. The Thurlows have a long and continuous history, reaching back to at least Roman times, and were mentioned in Domesday in 1086. The landscape is what passes for 'rolling' in Suffolk, the two villages set in a shallow valley formed by the last glaciation. The soil is heavy boulder clay over a base of chalk and is farmed mainly for arable crops, though cows are also pastured on suitable meadows down by the river. The River Stour is a key environmental feature. It rises nearby and runs through both villages, later forming the county boundary between Suffolk and Essex, until it reaches the North Sea at Harwich some 60 miles away, as the otter swims.

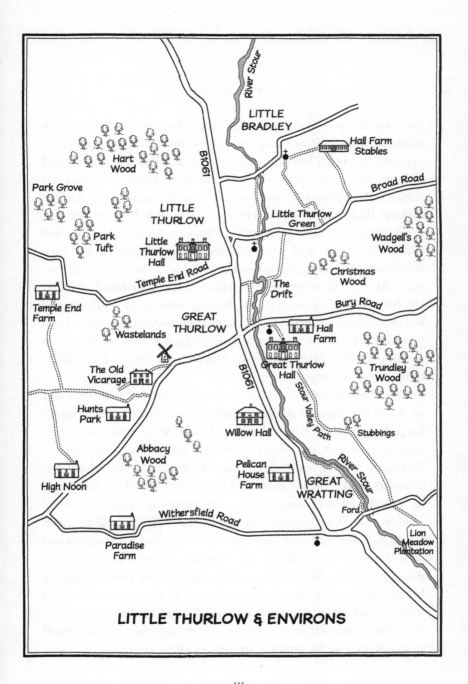

LITTLE THURLOW & ENVIRONS

Peter Marren

Peter Marren is the author of over twenty books on natural history and the countryside, military and entomological history, and bibliography, including *Bugs Britannica* (2010), *Rainbow Dust* (2016) and *Chasing the Ghost* (2018). He won the BSBI Presidents' Prize for *Britain's Rare Flowers* (1999), which was also runner-up for the Natural World Book Prize. He was also awarded the Society for the History of Natural History's Thackray Medal for *The New Naturalists* (1995), and won a Leverhulme Scholarship for *Bugs Britannica*. He had a column in *Countryman*, as well as the thirty-year-old cult 'Twitcher in the Swamp' column in *British Wildlife*. He has written for most of the leading national newspapers and has professional experience of nature conservation in England and Scotland. He is the author of *Nature Conservation* in the long-running Collins New Naturalist Library, and has co-led wildlife tours in many European countries.

Peter's patch is the Wiltshire village of Ramsbury in the valley of the River Kennet in the North Wessex Downs. The village has a long history, dating back to Saxon times when it had its own bishop and ten water mills, far more than Swindon or Newbury (which only had two). Fortunately, the place was bypassed by the main road, the canal and finally the railway, and so remains what it always was, a village at the centre of a large rural parish. The countryside above the valley is rolling chalk downland, mainly under crops but with scattered small copses and natural chalk grassland on the steepest slopes. The river runs through wet meadows, willow scrub and reedbeds from Ramsbury Manor in the west and Littlecote House in the east, each seated within their parks. Numerous footpaths and bridleways connect the village with outlying settlements, although the riverbank itself is mostly private to preserve its famous trout fishery.

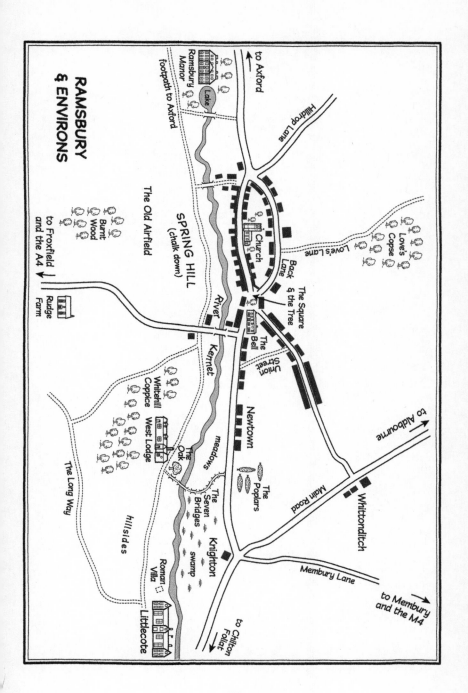

'There is something to be wondered at in all of nature.'

Aristotle
Parts of Animals, 645a17

Introduction:
Spring in the Time of Coronavirus

Michael McCarthy

If there was one mitigating circumstance about the coronavirus pandemic that hit Britain and most of the world in 2020, killing thousands of people, imprisoning millions more in their own homes and devastating national economies, it was that the virus struck in the early part of the year. It hit when the world, at least in the northern hemisphere, was entering into springtime. It is not difficult to imagine how the strain of bereavement for many, illness for many more and lockdown for virtually everybody would have been intensified if, as the first wave of the pandemic progressed, we had all been progressing with it into the dark and cold and wet of November and December. As it was, we were moving towards April and May, towards the warmth and the light, and that offered some hope.

The coronavirus spring that followed turned out, in fact, to be a remarkable event, not only because it unfolded against the background of the calamitous disease, but also because, in an extraordinary conjunction, it was in Britain the loveliest spring in living memory. It had more hours of sunshine, by a very substantial margin, than any previous recorded spring; indeed, it was sunnier than any previously recorded British summer, except for three. It meant that life in the natural world flourished as never before, just as working life in the human world was hitting the buffers, with a resounding crash.

The coincidence of these two remarkable circumstances is what this book sets out to record, but its ultimate aim is more than documentary; in illustrating the worth of nature at a particular, crucial moment, the moment of the Covid-19 pandemic, it seeks to highlight its worth as a whole.

The book came about because I discovered that my fellow nature-watchers Jeremy Mynott and Peter Marren had been recording the spring as the virus progressed, just as I had been, with the difference that they both lived in the countryside, in East Anglia and Wessex respectively, while I lived in the London suburbs. My two old friends were each looking at what birdwatchers call their 'patch', the local area they seek to monitor most closely for wild-life sightings. In Jeremy's case this was the farmland around the Suffolk village of Little Thurlow, and in Peter's, the chalk downland and the associated valley of the River Kennet near the Wiltshire village of Ramsbury. My own patch was somewhat different: it was the Royal Botanic Gardens, Kew, where I have spent many years gazing as much at the native wildlife as at the splendid horticulture and the botanical treasures from across the world. But the day before the lockdown was declared, Kew Gardens closed for the pandemic's duration, and I was obliged to find other places to which I could walk to watch the spring unfold – non-essential motorised travel for any sort of distance being prohibited. Since I lived in Richmond upon Thames, eight miles from central London, I began to walk the towpath of the river, and Richmond Park, the largest of the royal parks, and also the suburban roads on the borders of Richmond and Kew, to see how much of the seasonal change could be observed in an urban setting (a very leafy one, let it be said).

I had never recorded a spring before, I mean, not in detail, although Jeremy and Peter had been recording nature for decades. I have loved wildlife and the natural world since I was a small boy, but I have never kept a regular calendar, like they have done, and written down religiously that the first celandine flowered on this day, and I heard my first chiffchaff sing on that day and saw my first brimstone butterfly the day after. Yet this spring, the Covid spring, was different; it seemed unlike all others, not least because, in southern England anyway, it was proving exceptionally beautiful, yet by unfolding in parallel with the disease it was producing a sort of bizarre and tragic incongruity. Our beloved summer migrant birds, the swallows and cuckoos, the swifts and the willow warblers, were returning from their winter in Africa; the spring butterflies, the brimstones, the orange-tips and the holly blues, were emerging with their flashes of brilliance; and the spring flowers, the celandines, the primroses, the lady's smocks and the bluebells were each day adding new colour to the landscape, which was only intensified by the sunshine which from morning till evening seemed to pour down uninterrupted. Yet even as all this was happening, people were dying every day in their hundreds from the virus, often away from their loved ones, alone and in distress, and not a few of the health workers and care workers who were trying to save them were also dying, while millions of others were struggling to cope with the loss of jobs and the stress of being confined to their homes, especially if home meant a small flat. You almost felt that nature should have switched off, out of sympathy. Yet nature went blithely forward, as nature has always done.

This paradox was what made this springtime unique, and made me feel that it required memorialising; and I was writing it down, following its development day by day. When I found that my friends – both far better naturalists than me – were writing it down as well, I suggested that we record the spring together, and combine and compare our records in a joint narrative, and they readily concurred. We agreed to start at the spring equinox in March, the beginning of the astronomical spring, which by chance immediately preceded the nationwide lockdown ordered by Boris Johnson, the prime minister, in an attempt to halt the British part of the pandemic. We would finish at the end of May, the conclusion of the meteorological spring, because these ten weeks hold the vast majority of the changes in this most dynamic of the seasons. We also agreed that there would be an entry for each day by at least one of us. In the event, these covered a wide range of taxa and topics, from swallows to musk roses, from yellowhammers to mining bees, and from the imagination of George Eliot and the verse of Robert Herrick to the ventriloquial abilities of the grasshopper warbler; and I doubt that few, if any, readers of this book, however great their expertise in natural history, will be familiar with the munching marsh marigold moth.

As the spring evolved, so did the pandemic, and we observed both; in our narrative, the events of the natural world are set against the progress of the disease, and the government's attempts to manage the unprecedented situation in which the country found itself. Yet there was something more: spring in the time of the coronavirus felt not just unusual, not just paradoxical and incongruous in its character, but *important* somehow. It seemed to matter greatly, in some way I couldn't at first quite put my finger on. There was something in the background, something about what this spring meant for the natural world and how people treated it, what it meant for human relations with the environment as a whole.

What we all three could see, initially, was solace: it was clear that nature at its loveliest and most inspiring, in springtime's wondrous transformations, could offer people comfort at a moment of tragedy and great stress. 'There is no salve quite like nature for an anxious mind,' said Richard Deverell, the director of Kew, reluctantly closing his botanical garden as the pandemic took hold. A large number of others who had ready access to the natural world agreed with him, especially those with the countryside on their doorsteps, and wished to share their experiences of it, often using social media. Prominent among them were nature writers, in that rich modern tradition which has sprung up in Britain in the last twenty years or so. Mark Cocker, one of the most accomplished, tweeted on 18 April: 'I'm posting an uplifting image each day till this thing is done. No coronas, no Covids, but possibly corvids' (the last word a reference to one of his best-known books, *Crow Country*). Mark Avery, Britain's most influential wildlife blogger, organised a nature writing competition through his website. Melissa Harrison, crafter of moving novels about the natural world, created a series of podcasts about nature around her

Suffolk village. Some of our most brilliant wildlife photographers, such as Bob Gibbons and Richard Steel, began sending out inspiring daily images. Many others undertook similar enterprises. Jeremy, Peter and I were somewhat different: we were not publishing daily bulletins, but we saw the chance, in our recording, to put together an unusually detailed portrait of a particular springtime, which we instinctively thought could prove a source of consolation in similar difficult times.

The idea of the consoling power of nature goes back many centuries, but it is strange how relatively recent is our discovery of one particular aspect of it – the fact that the beneficial effects of exposure to the natural world on our physical and mental health are empirically real, and can be seen as such even in an era which demands scientific evidence. They had long been supposed, in a sort of obvious, generalised, sometimes slightly patronising way – *of course a walk in the park will do you good, like a nice cup of tea* – but it was not really until 1982 that we began to open our eyes to the true dynamic character of the link between nature and our psyches, with the publication of Roger Ulrich's celebrated paper in the journal *Science*, with its title of staggering banality and revolutionary implications: 'View Through a Window May Influence Recovery From Surgery'.

Ulrich was an American architect who specialised in hospital design, and in a hospital in Pennsylvania he had discovered something uncanny: over a period of nine years, patients who underwent gall bladder surgery made substantially quicker and better recoveries if they had a natural view from their beds. Some of the windows of the hospital wing looked out onto a group of trees and some onto a brick wall, and those lucky enough to have the tree view, Ulrich found, recovered faster, spent less time in hospital, required fewer painkillers, had better evaluations from nurses and experienced fewer post-operative complications than those who only had the wall to look at. The data were indisputable: they showed that contact with nature, even if only visual, clearly had a measurable effect on people's well-being.

Ulrich's paper is still not widely known by the public at large, but in highlighting the reality of our organic bond with nature, it seems more of a milestone in human affairs, more seminal with every year that passes; and since its publication, research has mushroomed into the effects of exposure to the natural world on our physical and especially our mental health, and there is now a vast literature. Such exposure is increasingly part of clinical practice, and recently in Britain a stream of books have borne witness to its effects, such as *Bird Therapy* by Joe Harkness, *The Natural Health Service* by Isabel Hardman and *Losing Eden* by Lucy Jones.

What all these accounts have in common is the belief that contact with the natural world reduces stress; and with the whole population confined to home, stress was one of the pandemic's principal consequences. The level of stress in those first weeks of lockdown depended on your circumstances. It was greater if you were poor than if you were rich: it was substantially harder to self-isolate in a small high-rise flat than in a mansion. It was greater if you were self-isolating with people who were difficult, such as demanding children or abusive partners – indeed, with the latter it could be dangerous or even fatal. It was greater if you were on your own, without support networks. It was greater if you were from a black, Asian or minority ethnic family, as it began to appear that people from a BAME background, for reasons that were initially unclear, were more vulnerable to the virus. But for most of the 66 million people of the United Kingdom, now being dragooned and bossed about in a way unknown since the Second World War, there was some level of strain and anxiety brought about by the abrupt ending of normal social intercourse, and the very real fear of infection.

In these circumstances, people sought diversion in all sorts of ways, but many turned to nature. It is clear their numbers were substantial. Let us take just one, astonishing figure: the increase in page views for the webcams run by the 47 wildlife trusts that look after nature on a county-by-county basis across Britain. Many people enjoy watching wildlife via webcams, which often show surprising and intimate moments at the nest or in the burrow. In the period 23 March to 31 May 2019, there were 20,407 page views of the trusts' webcams; but in the period 23 March to 31 May 2020, which corresponds almost precisely to the period covered by this book, there were 433,632 views, an increase of 2,024 per cent. And it was in contemplating numbers such as these that you could gradually begin to understand what was important about the coronavirus spring, besides its cherished ability to provide solace for the anxious. It was staring you in the face, but it was so simple, so obvious, that you were likely to miss it. It was the fact that it was there. The natural world was *available* to us, even at such a traumatic time. It had not been thrown off course, it had not been knocked out by the pandemic, by this great world-historical event that was knocking out everything else, that was making 2020 a lost year in human affairs. At this time of chaos in the world of people, nature was a constant, as it has always been. The Covid-19 virus had wrecked, if only temporarily, so many human artefacts; it had stopped business, trade, travel, sport, education, entertainment and social gatherings of all kinds – *but it hadn't stopped the spring*. In nature, 2020 was not a lost year. Just the opposite.

If you saw it like this, you suddenly saw once again the unique worth of the natural world, which produced us and shaped us, which holds our origins and which remains the true home of our psyches – as Roger Ulrich began to discover – and which even today, when so many have turned their backs on it, gives us everything, from the air we breathe to the water we drink and the food we eat. You saw anew its fantastic power and resilience. You saw its infinite value. You saw the wonder of it. But you also saw its vulnerability, because the coronavirus spring produced vivid instances of battered parts of the natural world prospering once more, of natural processes resuming when pressure from the mammoth human enterprise was temporarily lessened across the globe. Fish returned to the canals of Venice, no longer churned up by tourist boats. In parts of northern India, the Himalayas became visible for the first time in thirty years as air pollution fell. Baby sea turtles made it safely to the water on Brazilian beaches empty of sunbathers, joggers and dogs. Wild boar and deer came back into car-free European cities; in Llandudno in north Wales, wild goats roamed the streets. Some of these instances were in the nature of novelties, but others were significant: to give an example from my own experience, the historic landscape of Richmond Park in outer London was reintegrated and rewilded by the absence of the motor vehicle traffic that had previously cut it into pieces, and no one who saw it in that April, May and June will ever forget it. Most notable of all, the world experienced a colossal fall in the carbon dioxide emissions that are causing the most menacing of all our environmental problems, climate change.

Thus you can see the coronavirus spring, with its spectacular pause in human activity and its simultaneous flourishing of nature, as a great global reminder, a final warning that we have nearly reached the point of no return in our destruction of the natural world – we who in the last fifty years have wiped out half the planet's wildlife and started to destabilise the atmosphere. It is an historic moment. We are at a parting of the ways: one way, to continue as before; the other, to rebuild economies shattered by the pandemic differently, in a green way, above all so that climate change might be coped with and the natural world preserved (or at least as much of it as possible). And there are other lessons to be learned. One is: beware the consequences of degrading nature, as was done in the wet markets of Wuhan in China, the putative source (at least at the outset) of the Covid-19 virus. Another is: be prepared for major surprises, for the Covid pandemic was a surprise if it was anything, which the world was in no way prepared for; and some of the leading scientists of climate change, especially Wallace Broecker and James Hansen, have warned that the effects of global warming may not be gradual, as is generally assumed, but may be sudden and unexpected, such as abrupt changes in ocean circulation, or ice sheets collapsing, events that may catch the world out.

There are also lessons from the coronavirus spring closer to home. For in dealing with the consolation of nature, it is only right that we should ask: for whom was it available in Britain in 2020? For nearly everyone on social media, but for fewer of us in real life is the answer, although access to nature in some form was possible for more people than is implied by the official figures, which state that only 17 per cent of us in Britain live in the countryside, while 83 per cent live in towns and cities. This may be true, but it does not show the whole picture. Gardens, for example, make a big difference. According to a 2016 report on gardens and health from the King's Fund, no less than 87 per cent of UK households have access to a garden, and a lot of nature can be observed there. (My wife and I are probably typical; we have a forty-by-twenty-foot plot, less than two hundred yards from one of the busiest roads in the capital, but in it, during the coronavirus spring, we watched marsh marigolds and yellow flag irises come into flower, brimstone butterflies lay eggs, and goldfinches bring up their young.) However, that still leaves 13 per cent of UK households garden-free, which is a lot of people. How many of them had access to green space?

We can make some rough guesses. The Ordnance Survey produces a Green Spaces Index, which suggests that there are 2.6m people in the country who do not live within a ten-minute walk of a green space or park, 10,579 of them in London (though some of these people will probably have access to gardens). Britain at present has no official policy on how much green space should be available for its citizens. So perhaps one of the first Covid-19 lessons to be learned by the government – indeed, by all governments – might be to see that this is a gap which needs filling, and adopt the idea of the Green Party MP Caroline Lucas, who suggested in her 2019 general election manifesto that no new housing development should be sanctioned more than one kilometre from a public park.

Jeremy, Peter and I need no reminding of how fortunate we were, they to be in the countryside during the pandemic, and myself to be in one of London's greenest suburbs. But we attempted to put our good fortune to good use, by walking out every day, notebooks in hand, to set down and share what many others could not witness, in this most unusual and, as it turned out, most beautiful of springtimes. It seemed like a serious business, not least with a background of so many deaths and so much heartache; to go out each day observing seemed like a solemn act, and I felt at the end of it all that it was almost like an act of faith. I know my two friends also held this seriousness of purpose; we have a common view of the worth of the natural world, and it was a privilege to observe this spring with them, with their inspiring knowledge and expertise in that old-fashioned subject, natural history. If by our efforts we can help to show that the consolation of nature is a consolation like no other, and that there is something in the natural world which, deep down inside us, we long for, even sometimes without knowing why, then our enterprise will have been worthwhile.

The Spring Equinox and the Lockdown:
21–25 March

A blossoming wild cherry, blackcaps and chiffchaffs singing, willow buds bursting, coltsfoot in flower, mating gnats and sallow mining bees, an effusion of spring butterflies, the blackthorn winter, a lost wild pear tree, the manners of birds, buzzards in the sky where the planes used to be, walking the Long Way, and the cheering effect of jackdaws

Saturday 21 March

Michael McCarthy: A day of high pressure and glorious sunshine after a sodden winter of downpours and widespread floods, and the Royal Botanic Gardens, Kew, look stunning. It's the equinox, the start of the astronomical spring (as opposed to the meteorological spring, which began on 1 March), and it would be a moment for rejoicing, but for the fact that the news could not be more gloomy and frightening: the Covid-19 virus is now spreading rapidly in the UK, with confirmed cases standing today at 5,018 and, even worse, deaths up by 56 to 233. In Italy, 793 people died today – terrible – and in Spain, 324. I'm keeping a tally.

Such a strange and tragic coming-together, all this death and suffering taking place at an inspiring time in the natural world – for this spring is turning out to be exceptionally lovely, especially at Kew, which is my 'patch' in birdwatcher terms, the place near my home where I seek out nature. I am an urban dweller, but not of the inner city; my town, Richmond upon Thames, is in effect a leafy suburb of south-west London, so the changes in the seasons are visible all around, even in a world of bricks and mortar, and my wife Jo and I are very lucky in having Kew Gardens close by. Kew is not only about horticulture; there is wildlife throughout its 300 acres, but especially at the southern end in its ancient bluebell wood (officially known as the Queen Charlotte's Cottage grounds). I have been to Kew every week since late January, and I have closely watched the rebirth of the year in terms of flowers, first the snowdrops, then the daffodils, then the celandines, and now the prim-roses. The bluebells are next: the floral highlight of the year, due next month.

But will Kew stay open? Will it still welcome its two-million-plus annual visitors in 2020? For the last fortnight, the coronavirus threat has been steadily mounting; on 12 March, Boris Johnson shocked the nation by saying it would mean that 'many families are going to lose loved ones before their time', and last Monday, 16 March, he recommended that everyone should self-isolate: don't go to pubs or restaurants, work from home. On Friday, he finally ordered the pubs and restaurants closed, but lockdown is not yet mandated; his libertarian instincts clearly make him reluctant to order a complete, official confinement. Like everyone else, I am above all fearful of the virus and desperate for us to overcome it, and will willingly do whatever is required of me, but I also strongly hope that Jo and I can keep coming to Kew to watch the spring progress. Is that selfish? I don't know. Many other people must hope the same. I simply cannot help my feeling for the spring, a sort of hunger that demands satisfying.

Today Jo and I walked to the bluebell wood; the Kew bluebells when they flower and cover the woodland floor are sensational, one of the highlights of our year. They seem like a violet smoke swirling over the ground with the trees rising out of it, and we invite friends to come and gaze on them, and celebrate with a picnic; huge numbers of people do the same. The plants are half grown now; the flowers will be out in about another month, I reckon, as will the white starbursts of the wild garlic, the ramsons, which grow alongside them. In the wood you can see one of the few patches of primroses in Kew, which today were dazzling, but what most pleased us, on the woodland path where it curves around near the border with the golf course, was a gean, a wild cherry, in wonderful white flower. It is the tree of A. E. Housman's matchless lyric:

> Loveliest of trees, the cherry now
> Is hung with bloom along the bough,
> And stands about the woodland ride
> Wearing white for Eastertide.
>
> Now, of my threescore years and ten,
> Twenty will not come again,
> And take from seventy springs a score,
> It only leaves me fifty more.

> And since, to look at things in bloom,
> Fifty springs are little room,
> About the woodlands I will go
> To see the cherry hung with snow.

Some people consider this the most perfect short lyric poem in English. Certainly it does justice to the splendour of the tree, which in Kew today was beautiful beyond your dreams. I so much hope that the gardens stay open, whatever happens, and the bluebells do not flower unseen. But quite probably, that is not to be. As we left, a chaffinch was singing loudly his descending scale with the flourish at the end, and it almost seemed like a thanks and goodbye from the Royal Botanic Gardens, at this strange and menacing time.

Jeremy Mynott: Spring equinox, the moment in the year when 'night equals day' and the forces of darkness and light are in equilibrium. A perfect metaphor for the conjunction of this wonderful spring and the deadly virus invading our lives. I head off in bright sunlight down 'The Drift', the lane opposite my house leading down to the river. A regular daily walk along familiar paths, thrilling to the sights and sounds of spring once more. Everything is the same, but nothing is the same. The natural world is flourishing, as ever at this time of rebirth and regrowth; the human world oppressed and imperilled. Delight morphing into horror and back again, like one of those visual illusions you can view one of two ways but never both together. I gratefully choose delight for now.

I hear my first blackcap of the year, a lovely clear fluting, pure as a mountain stream. A few blackcaps winter here now, but this will be a spring migrant, and almost a week earlier than usual – I've kept a diary of these arrival dates going back four decades. The chiffchaffs have already been singing here in Little Thurlow, our village in west Suffolk, since 16 March – and quite likely from earlier, but that was the day I first heard them on my return home from a literary festival in the Lake District, a celebratory gathering that already seems a world away and would be unthinkable this week. Things have moved so fast that it's hard to absorb the change – the first UK death on 5 March, ten on 12 March, but over fifty yesterday . . .

I refocus. The chiffchaffs. There must be at least four of them chanting *chiff-chaff* in the copses here today. I like some of the old country names that perhaps capture their disyllabic song better: *chip-chop*, *chit-chat* or *siff-saff* (a Welsh version). Other European countries hear it differently: *zilp-zalp* (German) and *tjift-tjaf* (Dutch) are both nice, but the specific name *collybita* is perhaps more imaginative: it means 'money-changer', that is 'coin clinker'. I realise that the clarity of these and the other birdsongs I'm hearing all round me is intensified by the lack of any traffic or aircraft noise. This is so rare in today's mechanised world that the silence has the force of a new and positive presence, a medium in which the natural world can more fully express itself.

In some ancient cultures, closer to nature and more governed by the seasonal cycles than we now are, spring was considered the start of the new year. The Romans called it *primum tempus* (first season), hence the French *printemps* and the Middle English *prymetyme*. This spring will be the start of a new and different year for us too. Many people, I suspect, will be finding great consolation and delight in nature, often for the first time in their busy and distracted lives. I shall seek new inspiration in it as well, not as an evasion or denial, I hope, but an affirmation. I've always loved the sense of intimacy you develop with a local patch by walking it time and again, and I resolve to observe it ever more closely this year to deepen the relationship. This may be the most precious spring we have ever experienced.

Peter Marren: The 21st of March: one of the grail dates in the calendar, the moment when, at last, day equals night, and winter starts to turn into spring (March 1st is too early, unless you live in Cornwall). This year, the moment is exact. From my front window I see that the willow buds have burst overnight, bright yellow dandelions and celandines spangle the verge, and the air has a softness to it that seems new, a promise of fine weather to come. The birds seem to have noticed too. The robin that has sung solo at dawn for weeks past has been joined by a chorus of blackbirds, tits, a wren and a chaffinch. And for the first time this year – much later than usual – I hear the see-saw chant of a chiffchaff from the bushes on the far side of the lane.

It would be one of the best days of the year but for the huge threatening thundercloud hanging over all of us. The virus is spreading. It is clear that we are in for it now: that many will fall ill, and some will die before their time, and that the rest of us must make serious adjustments to our lives. You feel the weight of it, the crushing sense that life is about to change unimaginably, that our social existence is suddenly defined by avoidance and boundaries. It is unsafe to touch another human being, to breathe the same air as a stranger. I am a naturalist, and instinctively look for parallels in the natural world. Like honeybees, we are co-operative animals, perpetually busy building and stocking our 'hives'. We are about to become solitary bees, like those beginning to appear on the verge outside, each pair alone in their separate burrows, with their pot of honey and their modest brood.

This cruel equipoise between a promising spring and a darkening future will define our times. We seem to have entered a mythic story of life and death, darkness and light, the renewal of nature set against its opposite, the decay of human hopes and happiness. Nature will be a great solace this spring. I am lucky in that I live in a village that still has its modest portion of wild places, its wilderness of sedge and reeds, the strip of woodland running along the river, and the fields that flood in winter (and are still flooded now). But nature is in fact everywhere, universal in its ability to thrive in man-made environments (there is more diversity packed into the brown land of former industries than on the average farm). Nature will carry on regardless, and, even shut in as we are, we can watch it happen.

I live in Ramsbury, a village in the valley of the River Kennet, a few miles downstream of Marlborough. I have lived here for twenty years now, in one of a short terrace of cottages overlooking the flood meadow of the river. Before Ramsbury, I was a nowhere man, living, as my parents did before me, in a multitude of places without really putting down roots in any one of them. Ramsbury made me a somewhere person. Quite by chance, I found in it a place of, in Housman's words, lost content. Ramsbury will be my cockpit in the time of coronavirus. I will tramp its streets and byways once a day and record its ordinary delights, the surprises nature flings at us, and the momentary encounters with the lives of other beings with whom we share our existence.

Sunday 22 March

Jeremy: The cases of Covid-19 infections are now growing ominously – over 5,000 in the UK, and dire figures coming out of Spain and Italy. Fortunately, it's easy to self-isolate here in the Suffolk countryside and I wander along some hedgerows bordering big arable fields. It's bright and sunny but there's still a keen north-east wind, a reminder that seasons don't start and end punctually. Is this what Swinburne meant in that much-quoted line, 'The hounds of spring are on winter's traces'?

Lots of spring flowers have been out for weeks, in the regular succession from aconites through lesser celandine, primrose, daffodil, and now also cowslip and coltsfoot – the latter standing out from the surrounding dandelions with their distinctive stalks sheathed in leafscales that are supposed to resemble colts' hooves. I don't quite see that myself, but it may be a safer aide mémoire than its older folkname 'cough-wort' (mirrored in its scientific name *Tussilago*). Coltsfoot was once taken as a herbal cough cure, but it can have serious side effects and shouldn't be seized on by anyone seeking a quick panacea against the current virus.

I wonder why so many of these early spring flowers are yellow? One suggested reason is that yellow is more likely than darker colours to be attractive to potential pollinators in these lower light levels and shorter days; their pale colours may also absorb what heat there is more efficiently. But then again, there are plenty of early spring flowers that are white or blue, and plenty of yellow ones that come later in the season, so there is no simple or single explanation. There will be more such wonderings and wanderings to come.

Michael: And today Kew closed, for the duration of the emergency. How many different ways can you cry, *alas*? Richard Deverell, the director, said in a statement: 'There is no salve quite like nature for an anxious mind. We wanted to keep our botanic gardens open for as long as possible, to offer our visitors a space of tranquillity and beauty at this stressful time.' But clearly the closure was necessary, as the virus is now spreading rapidly; the death toll was up 47 today to 280, and total cases up 665 to 5,683. It means that the Kew bluebells and the ramsons will indeed flower unseen in 2020, and the blackcaps will sing over them unheard by human ear; if we want to watch the spring at close quarters, we will have to go somewhere else.

When we found the Lion Gate closed, Jo and I turned about and walked across the Old Deer Park and down to the Thames, past Richmond waterfront and up through the Terrace Gardens on the slope of Richmond Hill (where the most spectacular of all the magnolias I have been gawping at this spring was in glorious bloom). There were plenty of people about – the government advice is confusing, with self-isolating still only a recommendation – and a fair amount of wildlife. The herons were nest-building on the big ait just downstream from Richmond Bridge (an ait or eyot is a Thames island), and by the quayside there was a pair of mandarin ducks amongst the mallards and the Canada geese. Male mandarins are spectacular: introduced from Asia, they look as if they have stepped straight out of a Chinese painting, with rusty-coloured whiskers and orange 'sails' on their backs. It wasn't a bluebell wood, but it was a start.

There are rumours on Twitter of a proper compulsory lockdown coming tomorrow.

Peter: This is my spring: the daily release, each about the length of a communion service. For communion is what it is about. After four months of the wettest winter in memory, I long to catch the awakening world in my breath, in my being, in my bones. I long for nature to put a spring in my step.

One looks for a symbol of awakening, of an affirmation from the wild. The path across the valley is still a porridge of mud, dragging on your wellies, turning every step into a slide. Yet two recent moments marked the start of the season for me. Small in themselves, they express the earth's awakening.

The first came when I was returning from a barbecue next door – by the look of things probably the last social event for the duration. By chance, the lane where I live is aligned exactly east–west, and is bordered by trees, a scruffy scrub of higgledy-piggledy willows and sickly ash. At that precise moment, the low sun was streaming down the street like a searchlight. By chance, its beam caught a swarm of tiny gnats, turning each of them into a minuscule spark, gilded by the setting rays. My neighbour blundered through the swarm, waving his arms. He doesn't like flies. Once he'd gone, the glittering stars settled back into the dance, up and down and around. Presumably the best dancers get the girls, though they won't have long. By morning, most of them will be dead, and the female gnats busy with their eggs. They were probably fungus gnats. They don't bite or sting. Their unseen maggots munch dead leaves all winter, cleaning up autumn's mess. I thought they were beautiful; a street party celebrating the coming of spring.

The other sublimity was the day the sallow tree over-looking the gravelled yard, our communal car park, buzzed into life. It had put forth catkins seemingly overnight: small green puffs, ripe with pollen, which unlike those of willows also contain nectar: the bee's reward. I had hardly seen a single bee all winter. Suddenly that morning there were hundreds of them, mere dots against the light, but making that steady, satisfying, audible hum we used to associate with midsummer meadows. A few were bumblebees, but most were much smaller: solitary mining bees. Where had they all come from? It was as if the very earth had exhaled a swarm, and the tree had attracted it like a beacon. They worked the tree all morning, catkin by catkin, and then were gone. I never saw them again. I think they were sallow mining bees, the earliest of bees and one that has come to rely on a single, admittedly bountiful, plant. Those tiny buzzing dots reminded me of an old word, *atomies*. They appeared not so much as individuals as a whirling mass of particles, animating the tree. That's often the case with insects: it's the swarm (or in the case of ants, the heap), not the individual, that becomes the entity. Though an everyday, commonplace happening (but wonderful to witness from home), it also seemed miraculous. It wasn't just the sudden onset of spring: to me, the bees symbolised hope.

Monday 23 March

Michael: So it's official: from tonight, we are all locked down. Boris Johnson, seeking to strike a Churchillian pose in a dark suit next to a Union Jack, tells us in a televised address at 8.30 p.m. that we all have to stay in our homes for the foreseeable future, to combat 'the biggest threat this country has faced for decades'. He instructs the nation: *You must stay at home.* Sixty-six million of us, the entire population, dragooned in a way unknown since the Second World War. What are people going to do?

I review my options for nature watching, which with Kew Gardens closed boil down to two: Richmond Park, the largest of the eight royal parks, whose nearest point is just over a mile away; and the towpath of the River Thames, a little closer. There is a further option, which is to observe what is going on around me as the spring progresses here in the suburbs. Ever since I read Richard Fitter's *London's Natural History*, first published in 1945, I have had an interest in urban wildlife, but I have never looked as closely as I should have done; now I shall. The garden will help. Gardens may prove the other lockdown life-saver. Britain is a nation of gardeners, and Jo and I are probably typical; our plot is small but well loved.

Earlier today, I bumped into Franko Maroevic, our local birder, who lives around the corner. Franko is fairly well known in the birding community and from time to time alerts me to local rarities; he sometimes birdwatches with his telescope from his roof, which he refers to as 'the Richmond bird observatory'. Today he said to me: 'The wheatears are arriving in Richmond Park.' I suddenly have in my mind's eye that terrific, handsome bird of the uplands and coastlands, which I always think of as bouncing around, so energetically active it seems on arriving back from its winter in Africa; it is one of the very first to do so, long preceding the swallows, the nightingales and the turtle doves. And I think, yes indeed, if the wheatears are arriving, so is the spring.

Peter: Spring comes late to Ramsbury. Cold westerlies from the Marlborough Downs funnel down the valley and ensure that temperatures remain several degrees lower than in Hungerford, only three miles away. We are a windy village. Exposed trees face regular blasts, and they show it, with limbs torn off and branches turned away downwind. A couple of houses along from me there is a larch with a bent top, as if it were growing on a mountainside.

Would it be tactless to talk about dying trees on a day when some of *us* may be dying, gasping for air, sweating helplessly beneath the sheets? But many of our trees *are* dying all the same. The gales are getting more regular, more hard-hitting. We are losing our specimen trees, the village landmarks. Near the square is a house called The Cedars, named after a great spreading tree with multiple trunks. Well, that cedar came down with a crash last spring. A poplar plantation just up the road toppled – or should I say poppled – like skittles when a gale struck it the January before last. Planted in the hope of selling the timber for matchsticks, the trees are now good for nothing, not even firewood, unless you count their negligible assistance in carbon reduction.

I am in mourning for the wild pear tree that hit the dirt only last month. You barely noticed it (the tree stood by a junction where your eyes are on the road) until, briefly every April, after the blackthorn 'winter', but before apple-blossom time, it burst into glorious flower, heavy and snow white over black bark. It was obviously loved, even though its small pears were woody and useless. It was a tree that had suffered in its youth: toppled or chopped at head height, it grew up again tall and narrow, its five vertical branches soaring from a single trunk. Those branches, it seems, were too much for the trunk to bear. Two years ago, a great wind blew and knocked down the outer two – its arms, so to speak. The tree became a spindly remnant of what it had been. And then the wind blew again, and down came the rest. It was, as far as I know, the only mature wild pear tree for miles around, and for a week in the year it was eye-wateringly beautiful. One of the reasons we love trees, surely, is their permanence, as landmarks spanning human lifetimes. We grow old, but a great tree simply matures. Yet as the climate grows wetter, windier, more violent, and trees, like us, succumb to new, imported diseases, maybe we will come to see them in a different light.

Jeremy: An effusion of spring butterflies in the warm sun today. A few of our butterflies overwinter, hibernating in thick ivy or in our sheds, and I've been expecting some of them to emerge any day. But here they suddenly are all together, tracking up and down this sheltered lane. They make a mobile spring bouquet of mixed blooms – brimstone (the male a bright sulphur, the female a much paler yellow, almost white), small tortoiseshell (a patterned orange, yellow and black), peacock (deeper brown, with those compelling iridescent 'eyes' on each wing) and comma (saturated marmalade).

This last is a special beauty, settling intermittently on a patch of bare soil, to absorb the heat from above and below. The comma's most striking feature is the jagged edge to the wings, but both its common and scientific names refer to a small semicircular mark on the underwing that you could easily miss. Viewed from below, this does indeed look like a comma on the right-hand underwing; but the great taxonomist Carl Linnaeus must have been looking at its reversed mirror image on the left-hand one when in 1758 he gave the butterfly the unusual specific name of *c-album* ('white c'). The sort of imaginative touch, perhaps, that induced his fellow Swede, the playwright August Strindberg, to say that Linnaeus was 'a poet who happened to become a naturalist'. For the most part, though, Linnaeus lived a life governed by industry, order and habit. The story goes that he went to his local parish church at Hammarby every Sunday accompanied by his dog Pompe. If he thought the sermon too long-winded he would walk out after precisely an hour; and if Linnaeus was too ill to attend, his dog would go in his place (and would also walk out after an hour).

Here in rural Suffolk, people are quite quickly changing the habits of a lifetime, however. I wasn't the only one enjoying the butterflies in this sunny spot today. Parents and children were pointing them out to each other, while manoeuvring to maintain a careful distance as they passed me, with many an apologetic smile and friendly word. The need for social distancing seems at this stage to be bringing communities together rather than dividing them, and encouraging, amongst other things, a shared interest in nature.

Tuesday 24 March

Peter. The lockdown descends with stunning suddenness. What it brings to the village, right away, is silence (the loneliness, the fear perhaps, will come later). On my daily walk, I pass along the high street as if in a dream. Our two pubs closed last week, but the post office remains open. We form a short queue. An old lady bustles out, clutching a hankie to her face. A chap with a white beard standing six feet behind me is fatalistic. If I catch it, I catch it is his view. He probably lived through the Blitz as a boy. At the other shop, up a side street, the shopkeeper complains he can't find a mask to wear: they have all been panic-bought. The shop has also run out of loo rolls and soap. You wonder: can one catch it from newsprint, from unwrapped bread? You return thinking, don't touch your face, *don't touch your face*. And then rush upstairs to wash your hands while singing 'Happy Birthday' twice (the recommended time indicator for the washing).

The strangeness of our situation takes a while to sink in. It has never been this quiet, not even at night. The background noises – the distant rumble of the motorway, the aircraft in the sky, the more proximate sounds of traffic – are gone, and I can hear a wren singing in the churchyard, the hum of mining bees on the verge, blackbirds quarrelling from behind a wall. The birds seem to be singing more loudly, their notes more sharply accentuated. They aren't, of course. Our ears haven't yet adjusted to the new and surreal circumstances: the sound of England before the internal combustion engine.

When the Taliban took over in Afghanistan, someone had the temerity to ask what they were allowed to do now. No TV, no music, no sports, for women nothing very much at all. The answer they were given was that they could go out and look at the flowers, the beautiful flowers. Yes, we still have that, England's wild flowers, as beautiful as anywhere in the world, all around us and seldom given more than a glance. I am going to look at flowers this spring. Really look at them.

Jeremy: We are allowed outside for one walk a day to exercise, so I make mine a long one, hoping to exercise more than just my legs. I meet only one other person, someone I've never seen out on a walk before, let alone on a weekday. From a safe distance he shouts, 'Wonderful to hear the silence, isn't it?', not seeing the irony. He also gestures at the hedges bordering the track, 'Tremendous blossom this year'.

The blackthorn is indeed in full bloom, forming a brilliant white corridor across the fields, like a dazzling band of fresh snow. And since there is still a persistent northeasterly wind we enjoy repeating to each other the old country saw about a 'blackthorn winter'. Historically, it's been an easy conjunction to predict, of course, since the blackthorn usually flowers for some weeks in March and April, and winter would often reassert its iron grip in that period. The nineteenth-century Scottish meteorologist Alexander Buchan claimed to have identified a systematic pattern to these bitter spells, which became known as 'Buchan's cold snaps', but he made the mistake of being too precise about it, giving 11–14 April and 9–14 May as his dates for the cold snaps. He may have won credibility by sometimes being right, like a canny fairground fortune-teller, but it was in fact pretty random. In any case, Buchan knew nothing of climate change. We've scarcely had a winter in East Anglia this year, certainly not an old-fashioned freeze-up, just a handful of frosty nights. But no doubt the proverbial invocation of the blackthorn winter will survive as a metaphor celebrating the blackthorn's dense drifts of white blossom, even as we redefine winter itself to suit the changing meteorological facts. The new blackthorn winter of snowy blossom in spring weather may presage the next impending crisis the world faces.

Michael: Well, we are locked down for the foreseeable future, but on this our first day of it there was a compensation: the sunshine was so intense that Jo and I had lunch in the garden. We've been in this house for twenty-six years and I don't think we've ever done that in March before, not once; but something even more remarkable then happened. I suddenly heard a mewing noise, high in the sky, and sat up straight. I said to Jo: 'That's a buzzard!' If you know the sound, you can't mistake it − as a boy I learned to imitate it with a broad piece of grass stretched between my thumbs. I was facing the wrong way and couldn't see, but Jo looked up and cried: 'There's two of them!' and I twisted and dragged myself upwards just in time to see a pair of soaring broad-winged silhouettes, maybe a thousand feet up, disappear behind the roof of the house. I was amazed. Buzzards overhead here! But then it dawned on me − the planes have gone.

We live directly underneath the main flight path into Heathrow Airport, which is a mere seven miles away, and fully laden jumbos go right over our heads at 1,800 feet with their wheels down. The noise is thunderous. If you live under the flight path you simply have to accept it, although it's still hard to get used to the fact that if we have people for lunch in the garden in summer we have to stop talking while a plane goes over, and at peak times it's one every ninety seconds.

But there is not just one flight path into Heathrow, there are two, and the other one is parallel a mile to the north, passing right over the main entrance to Kew Gardens. This means that there is a corridor of deafening noise two to three miles wide, over more than ten miles of west London; and not many buzzards are ever going to fly into that, are they, still less go anywhere near a giant four-engined raptor. But today there was nothing. Complete quiet, complete peace. I simply hadn't registered that with the Covid crisis, international aviation has wound right down, and the planes have virtually disappeared. Great for us, but I wonder what else might appear in terms of birds, in a sky no longer torn apart by noise.

Wednesday March 25

Jeremy: A loose flock of fieldfares fly up from the meadow by the river. Maybe forty or fifty of them, chack-a-chacking loudly. They settle briefly at the top of some tall willows, looking nervy and agitated, but they have instinctively preserved some sort of order in one respect at least. They are all facing the same way, like so many flickering compass points. I don't say this is an invariable trait, but it's certainly a noticeable one. It strikes me as rather different from the way redwings, the other of our regular 'winter thrushes' from Scandinavia, tend to behave. Redwings usually settle in trees or bushes at a lower level, where they are much less visible; they then take off in a rapid, dodging flight in various directions – more of a disorganised party than a flock.

I recall a phrase from my very first bird guide, Edmund Sandars' *Bird Book for the Pocket* (1927 – the date of publication, not my boyhood!). Under each species description, Sandars had a nice little section which he called 'Manners', meaning the bird's distinctive habits or characteristic behaviour (a charming designation, more in keeping with that gentler age than today's functional term 'jizz'). Sandars' notes on the fieldfare's manners included this line, which stuck in my memory, 'All face the same way when feeding or perching.' There were many other vignettes of the same kind, some sharply observed, a few more dubious:

Mistle thrush: when disturbed, rise successively in a line.

Green woodpecker: has a strong pungent smell; energetic, watchful for enemies when boring, dodges behind trunk. Sometimes takes two or three backwards hops.

House sparrow: quarrelsome, bold, fussy. Nuptial display of throat with drooping wings. Tears yellow flowers.

Spotted flycatcher: sits on favourite perches in defined area, dashes out to snap insects (audibly); fearless, listless and depressed looking.

Water rail: fights a gull by turning on its back.

Hen harrier: great rat-catcher, very strong, kills blackcock with a single blow.

Well, hen harrier killing blackcock, there's a conservation dilemma we weren't challenged by then. The book has many other marks of its time: it describes as 'regular' species red-backed shrike, cirl bunting, Kentish plover, wryneck and corncrake, all now extinct or nearly so; and there's no hint that the turtle dove, corn bunting and cuckoo might soon become endangered birds; no mention either of such now-common species as little egret, collared dove or even Canada goose. But this is to read my much-loved book with twenty-first-century eyes. What it did then was capture my child's imagination with its vivid descriptions of the birds of the gardens, woods and fields around me. It was a guide in a true sense; not a book of instruction, but a way into a natural world I could begin to discover and describe for myself. A creative gift for these desperate times, as we learn that infections have now surged to nearly 10,000.

Peter. Today, with the sun at full strength and the wind having a rest for once, I walk the Long Way. This takes me across the wet meadow on the path known as Seven Bridges – because it has that number of wooden bridges crossing successive field drains and, finally, the river. I then follow the track to Littlecote, skirting the strip of oaks and ashes that lies between the river and the open fields. From there the path joins a concrete track, built by American airmen in 1944 and used by farm vehicles ever since. It follows the swell of the downs, eventually joining a more ancient bridleway, passing up the hill to Whitehill Copse and back again into the village. It's about four miles.

As in much of England, our good bits are small, scattered and tucked away. One such is a patch of willow scrub currently occupied by a lurking Cetti's warbler. Its explosive splutter of high-pitched squawks erupts from a seemingly empty bush. Another good spot is the primrose patch, with its accompanying retinue of little green moschatel flowers, from where you get a good view over the marshes.

The best bit of all is the path through Whitehill Copse, where it forms a hollow way, deepened by wagons over hundreds of years, running between mossy wood banks. You hear the repetitive *hwit* of a nuthatch from a tall beech.

You spot the first violets and sense the gathering quiet and that vaguely earthy smell of old woodland (and the even fainter sweetness of opening buds). And then it is out again into the light, and the view of distant rooftops and chimneys, and hearing the bleat of newborn lambs. In former times I would stop on the way back for a pint at The Bell. If only.

Others are out and about too, on foot, or on bike, or exercising the dog, seeing in the spring and doubtless trying to forget the news. Someone asks, have you heard a cuckoo? No, not yet. But I do see rooks and jackdaws busy building or repairing their nests (and better corvid than Covid, say I), and hear stock doves with their weird *woo-ah, woo-ah* cooing. And so back home on the traffic-free lane, walking in the middle just for the hell of it.

Michael: Yesterday we were struck by the coronavirus-induced absence of planes; today it was the absence of cars. As part of trying to do our shopping safely, just after 8 a.m. Jo and I drove to the big Asda store on the A3 at Roehampton to do a 'click and collect' pickup of groceries she had ordered earlier, and on the way back we stopped at the Roehampton Gate of Richmond Park to do our daily exercise. We won't do it again – in future we will walk there – but as we were going right past, the temptation was too great. We left the car in a side street as the park is now closed to traffic, but we found when we went in that the effect was wonderful – on a heart-stoppingly beautiful morning, the absence of motor vehicles, which normally cut through the park in four different directions, made the landscape peaceful and lovely beyond belief, no doubt like it was in 1637 when Charles I enclosed it with a wall eight miles long, which still survives. I think when all this is over, the calls to ban vehicular traffic from the park completely will be strong. There were, however, plenty of cyclists, walkers and runners.

We walked up through the oak grove by the path that leads to the Sheen Gate, and everywhere jackdaws were building nests, picking up twigs and leaves in their beaks and taking them in to tree holes. It's a cop-out to anthropomorphise, but they do seem such cheerfully industrious birds, as do rooks, if you've ever seen them nest-building in a rookery. No rooks in Richmond Park (although there are plenty of carrion crows); they like to feed in ploughed fields, so to find them you've more or less got to go into the countryside, beyond the M25. But for today, with Covid deaths up to 465, and new infections up by a record 1,452 to 9,259, jackdaws will suffice – any cheerfulness is welcome.

2

When Spray Beginneth to Spring:
26 March–1 April

*Ash, oak and elm buds opening, a dipper that's not a dipper,
Jack flowers and Willie flowers, synchronised swimming by
great crested grebes, three different scavengers contesting a
corpse, skylarks ascending, red kites in London, wayfaring
trees and traveller's joy, cuckoo bees, the importance of cowpats,
and a rescued oil beetle*

Thursday 26 March

Peter: It must be a psychological consequence of the lockdown. I find myself observing the spring more closely than
ever before: the things that govern its momentum, define
its progress. For perhaps the first time in my life, I watch
the leaves unfurl, day by day. On every tree the process is
different. Ash, for example, begins with a flower burst, in
this case a brush of purple-tipped stamens at the tip of the
twigs. The tree's tender young leaves appear later, feather-
like at first, pushing from anterior buds in a shuttlecock
before angling stiffly outwards on their long petioles.

The leaves of oak, on the other hand, curl softly from
their glossy brown buds, half hidden behind waterfalls of

37

yellow-green catkins (they smoke yellow pollen on still, warm afternoons). For a day or two the big hedgerow oaks take on an almost autumnal hue with a pointillist scatter of copper before abruptly turning spring green – that delicious new green that somehow fills you with happiness. Baby oak leaves taste pleasant: green chewing gum, lacking the bitter tannins that build up later on. Glancing behind me to make sure no one is looking, I nibble a few leaves straight off the twig, like a browsing deer.

We still have a few small elms – Ramsbury's many big elms all died of Dutch elm disease in the 1970s – corky-barked shoots rising from the still healthy roots. The elm's miniature flowers are a gorgeous purple-pink, woolly-tipped and emerging from sprays of fresh green scales. Within a few days, it seems, they change into seeds, equipped with flanged 'wings' so that they can twirl through the air after being shed. Field maple has proper flowers laden with nectar as a reward for pollinating insects. They are green, but arranged in attractive posies inside splayed deep red sepals.

Why have I never noticed the beauty of bud burst? This is the season in miniature, the spring we only see and appreciate if we take the trouble to stand and stare. I think we should look at small things more than we do. A garden of delights awaits us each spring in every hedgerow. And all we do is to walk on by.

Jeremy: I've just glimpsed the local kingfisher, speeding under the bridge in a blue streak. It goes so fast that you just see the colour-trail, as in a time-lapse photo, never a still image; and it tracks low over the water, following every twist in the river like a tiny guided missile. (Come to think of it, there was a 'Blue Streak' missile once – the MoD weapons taxonomist must surely have had a kingfisher in mind.) But unlike the speeding bullet that hits you before you hear the bang, you do get a split-second warning with the kingfisher, a short, high-pitched flight call, and that gives you just a moment to react.

Another villager approaches. He's narrowly missed the kingfisher, unfortunately, but is keen to tell me about a find of his own. He thinks he might have seen a dipper half a mile downriver. Well, that would be remarkable. Dippers are residents of the fast-flowing streams in northern and western Britain and are only very occasional visitors to East Anglia. I hasten to the location. It wasn't a bad shout, in fact. Just the other side of a small weir there's a plumpish bird, about the size of a song thrush, standing midstream; it has a white chest and is bobbing up and down in the current, feeding energetically on small aquatic insects – all characteristic features of a dipper. But it turns out to be a bird from a quite different family, a common sandpiper. This will be a summer migrant heading north, having stopped off briefly to rest and refuel here, an uncommon visitor to the village but not an unprecedented one.

I'm very grateful to have been tipped off, anyway. It's really striking how many villagers are taking a keener interest in nature and are wanting to talk about it in this strange new situation. Already today I've also been told about a buzzard on someone's garden fence (with a photo to prove it in this case) and a barn owl seen on an early-morning walk. Of course, many people have been more exposed to the natural world through their enforced restriction at home, and the lovely spring weather has helped. But it's more than that. As the national news gets ever worse – the daily death toll in hospitals has now exceeded a hundred for the first time – people seem to be reaching out for something positive and life-enhancing, not to ignore or deny the spectre stalking the land, but to counteract it.

Michael: You don't have to live in the countryside to follow the spring – you can do it in the suburbs, through the blossom in the gardens, especially somewhere like the borders of Richmond and Kew, where I live. Just as in the country, the blackthorn blossom comes out first, before other hedgerow flowers, the small white petals appearing in advance of the leaves so that the dark stems seem coated in sugar, here the magnolias burst open before anything else in my streets and roads and avenues (apart from a few winter-flowering cherries), and they are so conspicuous because they too bloom before their leaves appear. You notice the magnolia flower buds swelling even in January, and you watch them grow big and fat as lightbulbs before, in the last week of February, they pop, and suddenly the tree seems to hold a flock of white doves perching on every bare branch. There is one just like that today, right next door, facing the street, startlingly bright against the brickwork. They are so extravagantly showy that you search for a word to capture their essence and find yourself weighing up adjectives with sneering overtones – blousy? brassy? In Kew Gardens there is a magnolia grove that contains some astounding examples, especially *Magnolia campbellii*, the pink tulip tree from China – I thought earlier this month that it does indeed look as if someone has tied pink tulips to the ends of its branches. You can see it from two hundred yards away because no trees are yet in leaf.

Meanwhile the daffodils are carpeting the suburban ground, the commercial varieties, of course, bright bilious yellow and plastic-looking, municipally tamed (although the smaller, paler and much lovelier true wild daffodils can be found inside Kew). The daffs – I feel like calling them that – splash the verges of the Kew Road with colour, though to be honest, I much prefer the celandines that are there too, the unnoticed lesser celandines lying flat with their eight golden petals. The first sight of them, usually in March here, makes my heart skip a beat. I will have to look closer for wild flowers in the streets.

There was a 'national clap' for the NHS tonight. Most people in our road took part, coming to their front doors, clapping, cheering and some even banging saucepans. A definite feeling of togetherness, and of hope, after all the anxiety.

Friday 27 March

Peter: The prime minister has tested positive for Covid-19; so has his health secretary, and so has Prince Charles. Meanwhile, here in Ramsbury, Jack is by the hedge. This hedgerow Jack is healthy enough. He is green and white, and he smells of garlic. The plant usually known as hedge garlic, or, with an implied car crash of flavours, as garlic mustard, has also been known as Jack-by-the-hedge since the distant days of William Turner's *Names of Herbes*, compiled at the time when Henry VIII was dissolving the monasteries. When Jack's weed is at its freshest, with a topping of starch-white cress flowers above a tower of new green leaves, I think it is an uncelebrated beauty, especially when its massed blossoms stand against a dark bank, as they do on our lane.

There are several Jacks in the British flora. There is Jack-in-the-pulpit, a country name for our wild arum lily, or lords-and-ladies. There is also Jack-go-to-bed-at-noon, better known as goat's-beard, whose yellow flowers open only in the morning sunshine. Jack-by-the-hedge (or, in my county, Jack-run-along-by-the-hedge) has also been called Jack-in-the-green, a tribute to those white flowers emerging from their jungle of leaves. Jack could be Everyman, the way English soldiers were called Tommies. Or alternatively, perhaps, he is a spirit that inhabits plants, peeping naughtily from the arum's sheathed pulpit, or pulling the floral bed curtains when the goat's-beard calls it a day. Whatever his nature, he implies familiarity. Only common wayside flowers, the ones we see every day on our walks, are called Jack.

North of the border, Jack becomes Willie. Garlic mustard, for instance, is known there as sticky Willie, though it is forced to share that amusing name with cleavers or gooseg-rass, the one whose burred seeds stick to your socks. As well as sticky Willie, there is also sweet Willie, one of the northern names of the red campion (not to be confused with sweet William, a popular carnation, though both have pretty bright red flowers). Ragwort is stinking Willie. The sharp smell of ragwort is obviously not to everyone's delight, but the real reason for the insulting name, of course, is that the plant is poisonous, especially to horses that accidentally munch it in their hay. There is no truth in the tale that the original stinking Willie was William, Duke of Cumberland, who slaughtered good Scots at the battle of Culloden. The name is much older than that.

Michael: Today I did my first walk along the towpath. The Thames flows from west to east, more than two hundred miles from Gloucestershire to the North Sea, but just before it gets to London, at Hampton Court, it makes a left turn and flows due north to Kew, before turning right and resuming its east-bound course. This north–south stretch, which is eleven miles long, is one of the most fascinating parts of the whole river, because on its banks are at least ten historic houses – the nearest thing we have in Britain to the chateaux of the Loire. There is Hampton Court itself, then Strawberry Hill, York House, Orleans House, Ham House, Marble Hill House, Asgill House, Richmond Palace (or at least its remains), Syon House and finally Kew Palace, where George III retreated to recover from his madness, and which now sits inside the Royal Botanic Gardens.

But this section of the Thames (which has been given a name, Arcadia, that has never caught on with the public) is not just historic, it is also remarkably verdant considering how close it is to London. It flows between wooded banks for the greater part of its length, and so the towpath is fairly rich in wildlife. At Richmond we sit in the middle of it: the round trip from our house up to Kew Bridge and down the towpath to Richmond Lock and back is five miles, so I will be trying to walk that, but this afternoon I did about half of it, on the seventh successive day of cloudless skies. What an unbelievable spring, in so many ways. The tide was high (the Thames is tidal as far as Teddington Lock, three miles upstream), so there was less to be seen in terms of birds – many of them like the gravel banks that low tide uncovers. But on the water by Twickenham Bridge was a pair of great crested grebes in full breeding plumage, all chestnut ear tufts; they were fishing together, diving simultaneously like synchronised swimmers, a splendid sight. And I found to my delight that lady's smock was in plentiful pale flower along the bank. I came back through Richmond town centre, and by the station I saw the *Evening Standard*; the headline said: BORIS HAS VIRUS.

Jeremy: A sight that would have been inconceivable in Suffolk only twenty years ago. There were three scavengers contesting a corpse. The first was a buzzard, once common throughout Britain, but after relentless persecution by game-keepers in the nineteenth and early twentieth centuries, its range had become largely restricted to Wales and the west of England. Later attempts to recolonise were further hampered by the deadly effects of myxomatosis in the 1950s (so decimating its staple prey of rabbits) and by the impacts of organochlorine pesticides in the 1950s and 1960s (from which all raptors suffered by being at the end of the poisoned food chain). It wasn't until 1999 that the buzzard was finally reinstated as a Suffolk breeding bird, though they are now back in numbers.

The second scavenger was a red kite, a similar story, though a more extreme one. In the Middle Ages they were protected by royal decree, as they kept the city streets free of carrion and rotting food. But from about 1600 they were persecuted as inimical to game interests, and by the mid twentieth century the remnant population had been reduced to just a handful of pairs in Wales. These magnificent birds were finally rescued by a large-scale reintroduction programme in the 1990s that has seen them spread back to many of their old haunts, and they too have now returned to Suffolk, albeit still in very small numbers.

The third bird in my little tableau was a raven. This charismatic corvid, the larger relation of the carrion crow, has been slower to return, after an even longer period of absence. The last breeding record in coastal Suffolk was in 1869, and the species was virtually unseen in the county throughout the twentieth century. Now at last they are moving slowly back eastwards across England; occasional sightings are reported locally and they are rumoured to be breeding again in the east of the county.

All three species are now protected by law and it was wonderful to see them together in one spot. But I need to identify the corpse they were feeding on to complete this story. It was a pheasant (killed by a fox, I think). Over forty *million* of these non-native birds are released annually into the British countryside so that they can be shot; and it was mainly for the protection of this (scarcely wild) human quarry that the three native species above were systematically slaughtered for so long. Perhaps what I witnessed, therefore, was an ironic historical revenge of a kind?

Saturday 28 March

Michael: You can follow the spring in the suburbs by the birdsong as well as by the blossom. The dominant avian singers here are robins and blackbirds. Robins sing all through the winter, with their short, wistful warbles, but the blackbirds only start up their free-form flute solos as the days start to lengthen, and every year I walk along the tree-lined roads listening for the first. It's sometimes in late February, but this year my blackbird epiphany was in March – two weeks ago today, I walked out of the house at five to six, and all the blackbirds were singing loudly in the evening light. I heard half a dozen in less than a quarter of a mile, all on rooftops – two in our road, one in St Paul's Road, one in Lion Gate Gardens, one in Walpole Road and one in Pagoda Avenue. You could hear each one a good distance away. Funny how the special radiance of the low fading sun switches them on, especially if it's accompanied by that lovely stillness, as it was today – a stillness sliced through by the sweet liquid notes.

It was the first beautiful spring evening of the year for me, and I rejoiced in it. Philip Larkin captured the atmosphere perfectly – 'Light, chill and yellow, / Bathes the serene / Foreheads of houses' – though he went on from there to write about a thrush singing. We have some song thrushes, but not so many. We have woodpigeons roocoo-ing and jackdaws chacking overhead and jays squawking and ring-necked parakeets shrieking. We have great tits calling incessantly *Teacher! Teacher! Teacher!* and goldfinches with an unending slight buzzing chatter, and dunnocks – hedge sparrows as we used to call them – with their loud squeaky song like a shopping trolley, which I sometimes briefly mistake for a blackcap. All of those get louder as spring progresses. What we do not have is house sparrows, going *cheep!* Once the urban bird par excellence, they've gone from London and nobody knows why. Not one sparrow in our garden in twenty-six years.

Sunday 29 March

Jeremy: I spent a happy hour listening to skylarks as I walked this morning. There's something about this bird's soaring flight and its outpouring of sound that has moved poets, musicians and country people alike over the centuries. The bird is famously celebrated in Shelley's 'To a Skylark' ('Hail to thee, blithe Spirit!'), but there is a less well-known poem by the Victorian novelist and poet George Meredith which evokes the lark's song even better, in a series of wonderfully mimetic lines that begin:

> He rises and begins to round,
> He drops the silver chain of sound
> Of many links without a break,
> In chirrup, whistle, slur and shake,
> All intervolv'd and spreading wide,
> Like water-dimples down a tide
> Where ripple ripple overcurls
> And eddy into eddy whirls.

and end, perfecting the image:

> Till lost on his aërial rings
> In light, and then the fancy sings.

Meredith's poem inspired and provided the title for Vaughan Williams' composition 'The Lark Ascending', where the solo violin captures perfectly the ascending spirals of the lark's song flight in steadily rising cadenzas. The music lasts almost fifteen minutes, which is about the time the lark too can sustain its song, and has achieved the status of a national favourite, though one whose source is now largely forgotten.

This artistic adulation is an interesting case of how our attitudes can change over time. Skylarks are basically birds of the open steppe. You never see them near vertical structures like tall hedges or buildings, and they are unlikely even to have been present in Britain before the forest clearances in the Iron Age. They then flourished in our grassy fields, and up to the end of the nineteenth century were thought of as a great delicacy for the table. The scale of the butchery was immense, with some 400,000 a year sent to the main London markets alone, including deliveries of up to 30,000 in a single day. And on the day the Forth railway bridge opened in 1890, there was a grand celebratory dinner with an immense pie containing no fewer than 300 of them.

In the twentieth century, opinions varied. When migration studies revealed that the skylarks which ate the winter corn in Norfolk came over from the Continent, the local farmers in the 1930s decided they were not British enough to protect. 'SKYLARKS THAT SING TO NAZIS WILL GET NO MERCY HERE', a newspaper headline ran. In the event, their later sharp decline was caused not by our farmers shooting supposedly unpatriotic birds, but by the changes in agricultural practices those same farmers were encouraged to make after the war. There were more pesticides and weedkillers, fewer rough grasslands, fewer weeds and seeds, and less winter stubble and loose grain; and all these factors combined to reduce both the larks' food sources and their breeding habitats. The skylark has declined dramatically in numbers in Britain (by almost two thirds in a generation) and is now the object of universal devotion. It is a happy coincidence that on this day I was invited to join one of those chain emails exchanging favourite poems to lighten these dark days. One of the first ones I received back was the George Meredith.

Michael: Red kites have arrived here, and not just high in the sky, where Franko the birder saw one last week. Today Jo and I were returning from our walk via the town centre, and as we got to the A316, the main dual carriageway from central London to the M3, we saw a big floppy-winged bird flying in front of us, only about fifty feet up. I said, 'Look at that heron, it's low,' but then I put the bins on it and exclaimed, 'That's not a heron, it's a red kite!' It appeared to be on its way to Richmond Park and was probably coming from the Chiltern Hills, which begin about fifteen miles to the north-west, and where kites are plentiful after their reintroduction nearly thirty years ago. But what a place to see it, on the edge of Richmond town centre – the magnificent scavenger of Shakespeare's London has returned, if not quite to the heart of the city, then at least to the edge (we're eight miles from Charing Cross.) And then I realised, when we saw it, it was precisely under the Heathrow flight path, where nothing is flying. Is this the lockdown dividend for nature? – red kites back in London, like the wild goats that have appeared in the streets of Llandudno, and the fish which have returned to canals of Venice now that the cruise liners have gone?

Monday 30 March

Jeremy: I find my first flowering wayfaring tree of the season, its dense creamy-white flower head conspicuous in a hedge bordering a small wood on the ridge, where the soil is chalky. It's quite early for it to be blooming and it's one of my favourite hedgerow shrubs. I particularly like its wrinkly, finely veined leaves, which are downy white on the underside, hence its old country name, 'hoarwithy'. The present common name is a corruption of 'wayfarer's tree', and I like that association with walking, too. It was the sixteenth-century botanist John Gerard who so named it, and since he also gave us 'traveller's joy' (old man's beard) perhaps he had a special sympathy with ramblers.

We did a detailed study of the hedgerows in our village a few years back, as part of a comprehensive Suffolk Hedgerow Survey (1998–2012), designed to produce a kind of green Domesday Book for the county. It was quite a revelation how many hedgerow species we found here when we really *looked*. There were several ancient hedges with eight or more species in a measured length, which according to the much-cited Hooper's Law (multiply the number of woody species in a 30-yard stretch by 110 to get the approximate age of a hedge in years) suggested that some of these might indeed go back as far as Domesday. It's only a rule of thumb, of course, with many exceptions, but we're lucky to have any ancient hedges at all. The British countryside went through a devastating period in the 1960s and 1970s, when farmers were encouraged to grub out hedges and drain ditches to enlarge fields for bigger and more 'efficient' agricultural machinery. We lost thousands of miles of hedgerows, and with them a huge slice of our wildlife, for which hedges act as shelters, corridors, larders and homes – mammals, birds, flowers and insects, the whole interconnected chain of life. Many hedgerows have since been replanted, but you can't make an old hedge any more than you can an old friend.

Michael: I have discovered a wood! I feel the exclamation mark is merited. Not every day, after living in a place for a quarter of a century, do you find there's a wood around the corner – or at least three quarters of a mile away – that you never knew about. Its official name is East Sheen Common, and it lies just off Sheen Road, the A305, the old route from Richmond to Putney and Wandsworth and central London. But it's sort of hidden, and it's not sign-posted in any way, with the entrance proclaiming itself as the entrance to the Richmond and East Sheen cemeteries. Walk up a hundred yards, though, and suddenly you're in extensive woodland. The real thing.

There are lots of hidden relict woods like this in outer London. David Goode, the ecologist who used to run London's environment services, wrote a super book in 2014 called *Nature in Towns and Cities* (a very worthy successor to Richard Fitter's *London's Natural History*), and he has a whole chapter on these rich habitats, which in the late nineteenth century the expanding metropolis swallowed up but often did not destroy. In a felicitous phrase, he refers to them as 'encapsulated countryside'. The great majority of them are ancient woodlands – like Highgate Wood in north London, the best known – which means they have been there continuously since at least the sixteenth century, and where it's not trampled, the ground flora can be very rich – there can be carpets of wood anemones, for example.

Sheen Wood, which is what I'm going to call it, is not ancient. It's secondary woodland that has grown up on what in the nineteenth century was heathland and acid grassland, and it's been battered for decades by walkers and runners and kids on bikes, so the ground flora doesn't look great. But it's a proper wood nevertheless, mainly oaks, with an understorey of bramble at one end and holly at the other, and when I entered it today it was echoing with birdsong. The trees were still largely bare, although the greening was just beginning on a few, such as elder and hawthorn. It's a time that reminds me of the medieval love poem 'Alisoun', which opens:

Bitweene Merch and Averil,
When spray biginneth to springe . . .

At the far end of the wood is a gate into Richmond Park, Bog Gate. You've got to go through the wood to get to it, and it's the way I'll be walking. Is Richmond Park 'encapsulated countryside'? It's surrounded by urban development on all sides, but it's nearly 2,500 acres in extent. We'll see.

Tuesday March 31

Peter. Today my daily walk takes me past an earth bank that is home to thousands of mining bees. They appear towards the end of March, and on a warm, still sunny morning like today's you can sometimes find a virtual carpet of small bees moving just an inch or so from the ground. They return from their foraging trips with bulging yellow pollen sacks on their legs, like pantaloons. Each bee is seeking its own particular burrow among hundreds of similar burrows, eventually locating the right one by sight and wriggling down to the underground nest. The last thing you see is its fat hairy bottom disappearing into the warm, friable earth.

This bank is perfect for bees. The soil is dry and faces the sun. The bees themselves keep the vegetation open and loose, and so guarantee plenty of wild flowers and not too much grass. Grass pollen is no good for bees. Instead, they have their pick of dandelions and early speedwells, as well as a wall of Leylandii that provides shelter from cold northerly winds, along with masses of yellow pollen from its tiny cones. God knows what the mining bees' honey is like with such bitter and resinous ingredients. But it is obviously good enough for them.

I find that the only way to get close up and personal with bees is to use close-up binoculars. Mine are Pentax Papilio (*papilio* means 'butterfly'), which, by some miracle of optics — I gather it is something to do with a reverse prism — can be focused down to within a foot or so. At that range a small butterfly fills the view; a bluebottle can look positively alarming; even tiny bees take on colour and personality. Without such aids, one sees them only a swarm in which the individuals are lost in the mass. But with the help of close-up bins, you not only notice the details of their wings, bodies and laden hind legs, but also realise that there is more than one kind of bee present. A lot more, and not all of them are honest, hard-working home-makers either.

The trouble with identifying wild bees is that there are a lot of different species, often sharing the same bank, and many of them look much the same to a non-specialist. The task is made all the harder by the normal variation within a species, and the fact that males look different to females. Here, the only one I can recognise right away is the ashy mining bee, *Andrena cineraria*, which is grey and black and, like most of these early bees, wears a thick coat of hair. There is a different one with a ginger thorax and a glossy black body. It looks like Clark's mining bee, *Andrena clarkella*, perhaps the one that visited my sallow tree last week. So this is where it lives.

You have to feel a bit sorry for these bees. It might look like a good life, out there on their bank in the spring sunshine, with nectar and pollen all around on big friendly dandelion heads. But it's really a jungle. The proper bees might be well fed, but they are forever being stalked by a buzzing army of freeloaders. For every ashy or Clark's bee, there is a smaller, wasp-like little critter with a yellow-and-black-striped body and bright red antennae. This is a bee too, a nomad bee, so named because it does not build its own nest; instead it roams about looking for a suitable burrow into which to craftily insert its own egg. The nomad bee is an insect cuckoo that takes advantage of an unwilling host. Its egg hatches into a grub with a nasty-looking pair of mandibles that grabs the rightful occupant of the cell, turfs it out, and then takes its store of honey for itself.

That isn't the only one. There are other cuckoos present in the form of blood bees, with red-banded bodies; and also bee flies, which aren't bees at all but look a bit like them, with their round fuzzy bodies. There are other unidentified flies hanging about too, which I imagine are up to no good. The astonishing thing is that today, at least, there are more cuckoos than nesting bees. Those underground nests with their cells of honey must be buzzing with muggers and thieves. Just imagine what it would be like to have one set of hostile ne'er-do-wells in the kitchen, gobbling up everything in the fridge, another set sleeping in your bed, and yet another chasing your kids. And even that isn't the worst of it. The worst thing of all is the stylopid. I haven't yet spotted one. If I do, and witness its evil ways, it will merit a nature note with a 15 certificate on it.

Wednesday April 1

Jeremy: The cows have been let out into the meadows today. They've all calved now and the whole herd is at last allowed to leave their winter stalls and crop the grass, which is especially lush this year after those February rains. The presence of the cows back on the fields is another familiar sight, and indeed sound, of spring. Cows have been blamed for a serious contribution to global warming through their massive emissions of methane gas. That comes from both ends – belching and flatulence. A cow can produce fifty gallons of methane a day, and since methane emissions are over twenty times as powerful as those of carbon dioxide, and there are some sixteen million cows in Britain, you can see (and often hear) the scale of the problem. In New Zealand, which has much more livestock than we do, there was even talk of a 'flatulence tax' to help save the planet.

But I recently read a scientific article with the splendid title 'In praise of cowpats', which makes a rather different point. Cowpats feed a host of insects. Masses of flies and beetles arrive within minutes of a fresh, glistening cowpat hitting the ground – I could see them in action today. And these are followed by legions of others as the pat matures, decays and is eventually pulled underground by worms and dung beetles, so contributing to new plant growth. Each pat in open pasture produces in this way some 1,000 developing insects –and with an average output of six pats a cow a day, that's 6,000 insects a day or over two million a year. So, an important micro-habitat – or it would be if cows weren't now routinely treated with powerful drugs to destroy internal parasites, which can render the dung toxic for many other organisms too. Maybe an argument for eating organic beef to protect insect populations?

We now know how crucial insects are to the whole web of animal and plant life. They pollinate plants, provide food for birds and mammals, and are crucial to human agriculture and food supplies. It's been estimated that if all the world's insects were to disappear humanity would only last a few months and the earth would eventually become a vast compost heap, supporting only a gigantic blooming of fungi. We also know that insects (including moths and butterflies) are under great threat, largely from the pesticides with which we drench the land; which in turn partly explains why farmland birds have declined so sharply, and why that other traditional harbinger of spring, the cuckoo, is heard no more in this parish, since cuckoos feed principally on caterpillars.

Peter. Today I rescued an oil beetle. This great monster, fully two inches long and quite incapable of flight, had blundered from its patch of grass, toppled off the pavement, and was now nonchalantly crossing the road, perhaps hoping for better grass on the far side. Fortunately for it, there is not much traffic on our lane just now. I tried, as gently as I could, to slip it into the palm of my hand. After I replaced it on the grass, I noticed a drop of oily orange liquid on my hand. Far from being a thank you, it is the beetle's defence mechanism. The oil is slightly caustic and leaves a stain. It does not bother me, a big hairy mammal that does not eat insects, but it might well be enough to discourage a hungry bird.

This happens every year about now. Luckily for the beetles, a kind neighbour looks out for them and picks them off the pavement before they get squashed. Bizarre in itself, long, black and with useless tiny wing cases, the oil beetle has been compared with a fat man wearing a tail coat several sizes too small. Their oil is their only defence, but I have yet to see a bird take one; the oil would burn its throat. It is the same substance as that produced by the non-British blister beetle, a chemical that was once used to remove warts. But the truly bizarre aspect of oil beetles is their life cycle. Their eggs hatch into a shrimp-like creature called a triungulin ('three-claw'), which crawls to the top of a flower and waits for a passing bee, then jumps aboard with its three tiny claws. The bee unwittingly carries the creature to its nest, whereupon the triungulin wriggles off and begins to help itself to the store of honey. It lives there all summer and winter, until the full-grown beetle emerges into the light at the beginning of spring. One unlucky bee was seen with thirty pinkish triungulins clinging to it. The downside of this life is that oil beetles depend on bees, and perhaps even the right kind of bee. No bees, no beetles, simple as that. And unfortunately, there are more and more places with no oil beetles. I think my neighbour would be sorry to lose them. They might need rescuing, but they are big and funny as they bumble along with twitches of their knotted antennae. They are forebears of spring, as regular as cuckoos, and like cuckoos – and cuckoo bees – with something of the same workshy attitude.

3

Now That April's There: 2–8 April

The first orange-tip, Robert Browning's longing, yellow-hammers, the first brimstone, weasels, pond slime, birds of tree trunks, the flower carpet of a holloway, a silent supermoon, finding a colony of house sparrows, liverworts and horsetails, and telling leaves by touch

Thursday 2 April

Peter. The British are dying at the rate of 500 per day, winnowed from the living by the stamp of some defect: heart trouble, diabetes, or just the frailty of old age. Most of the dead, we learn, had 'underlying health problems'. But, you can't help wondering, how unhealthy do you need to be to have 'health problems'? Perhaps only the virus knows the answer to that. That is what is so frightening. Covid will find you out. If there's a chink in your armour, it will find a way in. It will know what to do.

As I wander down the lane to the village, there is a flash of colour in the gloom. I spot my first orange-tip! You wait for that glimpse of butterfly magic almost as impatiently as you wait for the first swallow. This butterfly, more than any other, carries the spring on its wings: that sunshine orange, the dappled green freshness of its hindwings, the purity of its whiteness. The effect is made still more brilliant against the backcloth of the green-and-white hedgerow. And unlike some butterflies I could mention, this one doesn't fly off. It ambles along at my walking pace, fluttering, sensing the air with its chequered antennae and, you imagine, searching earnestly with its coloured eyes. Orange-tips are companionable butterflies, denizens of lanes and byways, ignoring your presence, intent on their own business. They flutter, they settle, they sip and move on.

In milder places than Ramsbury they have been flashing their beacon wings for up to a week now. The odd thing is that I spot this one in the very same place (and at about the same time) as I did last year, where the lane runs below a scrubby bank lined with garlic mustard just coming into flower. It flutters purposely along the bank; being male, it is probably looking for a mate (it will have to wait; the males usually emerge a day or two before the dowdier females). Later on, there will be bright orange bottle-shaped eggs on the garlic mustard flower stalks: it will have found its mate.

You can tell people love the orange-tip. Look at its Latin name, *Anthocharis*, 'flower-grace', or its French name, *l'aurore*, 'the dawn', the butterfly with the rising sun in its wings. Or its old name of 'the lady of the woods' (never mind that the orange-tipped one isn't a lady, nor does it live beneath the trees). It's fanciful, I know, but in that moment the butterfly seemed like a beacon of sunshine at a dark and threatening time.

Michael: Chasing the spring in an urban setting is satisfying, but I can't help thinking about what I'm going to miss this year, and that's principally the summer migrant birds, not least the four with the most legends and literary associations: the swallow, the nightingale, the cuckoo and the turtle dove. You don't get those in south-west London; I can't walk to see them or hear them on my daily lockdown exercise. One thing they have in common is that they all arrive back from their winter quarters in Africa in April, and that's what makes April perhaps the most exciting month of the year: the new birds and birdsong, together with the new leafing of the trees, which is really an April phenomenon. It's the dynamic change that is so arresting and heart-stopping. I've always thought that the poet of *The Song of Solomon* was describing April when he (or it may very well have been she) wrote three thousand years ago: 'For, lo, the winter is past, the rain is over and gone; the flowers appear on the earth; the time of the singing of birds is come, and the voice of the turtle is heard in our land' (the turtle of course being the turtle dove).

The April change is particularly visible and beautiful in southern England, and people who know it and love it sometimes long for it when they are away. Take Robert Browning. He and Elizabeth Barrett were idyllically content in their fourteen years of married life in Florence, where they went for Elizabeth's frail health. They wrote copiously and produced their son Pen, and indeed, you can stay in the Casa Guidi where they were so happy until Elizabeth died in 1861; but one day, for all the civilised delights of living in the greatest Renaissance city, Browning can't help himself and he bursts out:

Oh, to be in England
Now that April's there,
And whoever wakes in England

Sees, some morning, unaware,
That the lowest boughs and the brushwood sheaf
Round the elm-tree bole are in tiny leaf,
While the chaffinch sings on the orchard bough
In England – now!

Friday 3 April

Jeremy: The seasons are still blurred, with summer arrivals and winter departures criss-crossing in the airport lounges. Down the Drift and along the river there are at least ten chiffchaffs and four blackcaps singing, some perhaps passing through but some making loud claims to summer territories; while in the trees beyond, a party of redwings are psyching themselves up for their journey north with that scratchy communal chorusing they do just before take-off. One of our year-round residents seems confused, too. I suddenly see a flash of yellow in the hedge, then a bird flips out to perch on a spray. A yellowhammer – lovely – and he has a mate, I see. But why haven't I heard one singing yet this year? They often start in late February and are generally in good voice by mid March. I've been listening out for them anxiously. These song patterns are very regular, and when you are finely attuned to a local patch you feel a nagging unease about unexplained absences of this kind. Well, these look like a settled pair, so let's hope he sings soon and catches up with the season.

Yellowhammers are charming little birds. The second half of their name probably comes from the Old English *amer*, meaning a bunting, so they are really 'yellow buntings' (as in the French *bruant jaune*). The first half is clear enough, anyhow. The males have brilliant canary-yellow heads in spring, with a paler suffusion of yellow on the underparts. To my eye, a much happier blend with the traditional palette of colours in the English countryside than the harsh yellow glare of the rape fields beyond.

Two of the yellowhammer's old country names point to other distinctive characteristics. They used to be called 'scribble larks' because their eggs are delicately inscribed with a loose series of wavy lines that look like even worse handwriting than mine. And the other old name is 'little-bit-of-bread-and-no-cheese', which is meant to be an imitation of the song, though that actually sounds more like the less grammatical 'little-bit-of-bread, cheeeeze' (a stutter followed by a wheeze). They should be heard singing this refrain tirelessly all summer along these hedgerows. As Julian Huxley put it, writing in the 1940s about feelings of national attachment in a time of war, 'The yellowhammer's song seems the best possible expression of hot country roads in July.'

We are said to be in a war, too, and also need reassurances. To recite these scraps of folklore may be thought to be seeing the yellowhammer through a haze of nostalgia, however. The countryside is changing. The rape fields whose colour seems alien to me have been here since the 1980s, so are already a part of a new tradition for others. And one remembers how the peasant-poet John Clare bitterly lamented the replacement of his familiar open-field landscapes with the same enclosing hedgerows naturalists now so earnestly seek to preserve and restore. Nonetheless, if the yellowhammer eventually joins the other local casualties of intensive agriculture like the corn bunting, the turtle dove and the tree sparrow, I can't just view that as an inevitable secular process. I feel these losses keenly as an impoverishment, not just another change.

Saturday 4 April

Michael: As well as blossom and birdsong, there is a third very obvious marker of spring's arrival in the suburbs: the brimstone butterfly. I saw my first one today, with great delight, flying over a front garden hedge in the next road. It's such a spring signifier for two reasons: it is very early, and the pure lemon-yellow wings of the male are very conspicuous. It's early because it overwinters as an adult. Butterflies have four potential strategies for getting through the cold and damp months of the year, based on different stages in their life cycle – as an egg, a caterpillar, a pupa or a fully grown insect. All four methods are employed by the 58-strong British butterfly fauna, though only five hibernate fully grown (the others that do so are the red admiral, the small tortoiseshell, the peacock and the comma, all members of the same family). As a wintering adult butterfly you don't have to go through any more transformations; if the early spring sun is strong enough to wake you, you are ready to fly at once, and so any of the five adult overwinterers can be seen on the wing in March, or, with the advance of global warming, even earlier. (On 12 February 2008, in the churchyard at Turner's Puddle in Dorset, Martin Warren, then head of the charity Butterfly Conservation, took a picture of a red admiral nectaring on a snowdrop, an image once wholly unthinkable.)

Thus the brimstone may well be the first butterfly you see in any given year. In addition, you can spot it from a long way off, so bright is its coloration. But the yellow of the male is not just bright; the colour is saturated: it could not be any more yellow than it is. Only a few of our butterflies display saturated colour like this: the Adonis blue is one, and another is – or was, until it became extinct in Britain – the large copper, which has wings of the most brilliant orange you can possibly imagine (You have to go to continental Europe to see it now.) To me, the brimstone is so bright it looks like a piece of sunlight that has become detached from the sun's rays and freed to wander, and like many people, I glimpse the first one each year with exhilaration.

Female brimstones, which are actually very pale green but look silky white, lay their eggs on two rather scarce related shrubs – buckthorn, which grows on chalky soil, and alder buckthorn, which grows on clay. Last year we planted three alder buckthorns, two in the rear garden and one in the front, in the hope of attracting brimstones of our own. Fingers crossed.

Jeremy: A small mammal dashed across the path in front of me the other day and instantly disappeared into the ditch. Well, 'dashed' isn't quite right. It *flowed* over the ground in a ripple of movement somewhere between a bound and a slither. Too large for a mouse, too thin and sinuous for a rat. Something lightning fast, with energy to spare and a hint of danger about it. I stood stock still and after a minute or two a small triangular head with black button eyes and little rounded ears popped up from the long grass and inspected me closely. I was clearly neither a threat nor a meal, so with a flick of its tail it vanished again. A weasel.

Weasels are the world's smallest carnivorous mammals, feeding mainly on mice and voles, which they pursue relentlessly down the narrowest of tunnels. Hunters can quickly become the hunted, of course, and weasels are themselves predated by cats, foxes, owls and birds of prey. It's a ladder of power, negotiated in violence. The word 'vermin' comes from the Latin word for 'worm', which is at the bottom of this chain, but it expresses the point of view of the top predator in the chain, which is us.

Weasels are often confused with stoats, but are much smaller and lack the stoat's trademark black tip to the tail. They weigh in at just six ounces (about the weight of a small banana) and have to eat voraciously just to survive, consuming about a third of their own body weight each day. They have no permanent home, preferring to lodge in the burrow of whoever they have most recently eaten. They only live two or three years anyway, and it's a life of constant hunger, stress and striving.

Children in towns have probably never seen a weasel, but some may know of it from the old nursery rhyme, which begins:

> Half a pound of tuppenny rice
> Half a pound of treacle
> That's the way the money goes
> Pop! goes the weasel

Great fun, but what on earth does it mean? Is it to do with the habit weasels have of popping up in front of you, like mine did? No, something much more obscure. It seems to date back centuries to a form of cockney rhyming slang, in which 'weasel and stoat' meant 'coat' and 'pop' meant 'pawn'. Poor people would pawn their coats on a Monday to get the cash to see them through the week, then buy them back at the weekend to have their Sunday best available. A different cycle of need and replenishment.

Sunday 5 April

Peter. Under a leaden sky, a cold wind blowing, I decide that this is as good a day as any to look at pond slime. The ditch by the side of the road is green with a flocculent floating gunk. To the tadpoles swimming beneath it, the stuff must appear like a murky sky, as though about to spit bright green rain. I collect a bit in my pond net, bring it home in a jam jar, and take a look at it through the stereo zoom microscope I keep in a cupboard in the kitchen.

I have to say that, even as pond slime goes, this isn't prime material. This is very low-grade gunk. The delight I used to take in microscopy as a boy was in large part due to its revelation of beauty in surprising places. There are wonders in the leg of a flea, the tongue of a fly, even the guts of a worm. The disgusting sludge on your slide dissolves into a microcosm, the world of single cells, shaped like stars, bananas, violins, boats (one of the commonest algae is *Navicula*, the 'little ship').

In this case I was hoping for *Spirogyra*, noted for its spiral chloroplast, its greenery contained in a twizzle of matter, like DNA. Or if not that, perhaps *Zygnema*, which has a chloroplast that looks like a tiny spider sitting inside each cell. But this stuff isn't *Spirogyra* or even *Zygnema*. The closer I zoom in, the duller it looks, green threads (filaments) without twizzles or spiders, simply turning into an infinity of dreary green cables as I up the magnification.

I know what it is: *Cladophora* or blanketweed. Road traffic has laden the ditch with so much exhaust-polluted, nitrogen-rich mud that its natural vegetation has been replaced with this beastly stuff. Just as fertiliser will ensure that one kind of grass dominates a field, so nitrogen oxides have enabled the blanketweed to make this ditch its own. There is, I note, more life in my sample, certain wiggling semi-transparent forms. Time was when I might have made an attempt to identify them. As it is, I find them faintly disgusting; an unwelcome reminder of the world of Petri dishes and medical laboratories. No, not just now. The microscope goes back into the cupboard, and the slime, along with its squirming inhabitants, goes back into the ditch. Another time, maybe.

Monday 6 April

Jeremy: Two resident birds that are doing very well here this year are the nuthatch and the treecreeper. I think of them as our local 'trunk birds'. They are both very expert and nimble tree climbers but they have contrasting physical presences and techniques. The nuthatch is a chunky bird with a steel-blue back and warm buffy underparts. The name comes from an Old English word meaning 'nut hacker', a reference to its habit of wedging a nut in a crevice and hammering it with its strong dagger bill to reach the kernel. It behaves like a little woodpecker, with the difference that it's the only British bird that can climb head-first *down* a tree trunk as well as up. (I worked in New York for a time and in my 'away patch' of Central Park I used to watch black-and-white warblers performing the same trick.) In fact, a nuthatch is so active and energised that it seems to swarm all over the tree it's exploring. Nuthatches have been scarce in the village in recent years but have now returned in numbers, I've noticed, and it's good to have their bold, cheerful presence again.

Treecreepers, by contrast, are very unobtrusive and easy

to miss. They are smaller and much slighter, with pearly white underparts and streaky brown backs to give them excellent camouflage against tree bark. And they do just what it says on the tin. They creep, climbing up tree trunks like little feathered mice – a short spurt, a pause to probe a crevice with their thin curved bills, then off again, working their way spirally up a trunk; at the top of their ascent they then flit lightly down to adhere, as it seems, to the base of an adjacent tree and flick the switch to start climbing all the way up again.

The two birds' vocalisations are equally contrasting, each somehow appropriate to its persona. The first sign a nuthatch is around is often a loud, cheerful tweet – or should we say *twet*, to distinguish it from the chattering output of Twitter. And the song is a rapid repetition of similar calls, slurred together into a nearly continuous and penetrating trill. The treecreeper on the other hand has a shy, wispy little call, easily lost in the susurrations of leaves in a breeze, while the song is a soft, dry trill with a pleasing little flourish at the end, like a signature. Meanwhile, in the percussion section the other side of the river, I can hear another trunk bird with a quite different technique: a great spotted woodpecker drumming out his own spring song on a favourite dead branch in a willow.

Peter: Today my daily walk takes me north of the village, up Love's Lane, the old road to Aldbourne, past the allotments and between banked hedges towards our largest wood, called, with logic if not imagination, Love's Copse. Most of the small woods north of the village are 'copses'; south of the village they are 'coppices'. Why they have two words for the same thing (for copses *are* coppices) is a mystery.

Love's Lane, too, is not what it might seem, a lover's lane. It seems to have been named after a medieval forebear with a farm on the lane, a man called Lof, perhaps pronounced 'Love'. (We have a Scholard's Lane too; not named after a school, though there was one, but for a family called Scholard.) As an old and once well-used route between two substantial villages, it is only by chance that Love's Lane is not a tarmacked road busy with traffic. Fortunately they found another way to Aldbourne, through a valley rather than over the hill, and so Love's Lane remained what it is today, an unsurfaced byway used mainly by walkers and bikers.

It is the warmest day of the spring so far, the first in which I've been able to walk comfortably in my shirt. As I enter the wood between banks thronged with early flowers, it feels to my winter-starved eyes like the moment in *The Wizard of Oz* when the film suddenly bursts into Technicolor. The lane skirts the wood along a sunken path. This is a hollow way, or holloway, a shady path worn down by the traffic of ages. Above it, leaves touch from either side, ash sprouting from ancient stumps, and tall arching bushes of hazel, forming a fretwork of twigs and branches against the blue sky. The contemporary writer, Robert Macfarlane, compared the view through a holloway to looking down the barrel of a rifle.

For some metres on either side the floor is a tapestry of colour, a medley of yellow primroses and celandine, white starry wood anemones and barren strawberries, purple patches of dog-violet, and bluebells just coming into flower with a curl of that piercing blue. I search for one of my favourite plants, and find just two of them, tufts of pale pink among the twigs and moss. This is toothwort, an early-flowering parasite of hazel roots. Being a freeloader, it needs no leaves. Its short stalk is waxy white, as cold as ivory, with fleshy scales and a row of pink tubular flowers, each with a projecting stigma like a fairy trumpet. In a couple of weeks, its spent flowers will swell into tough white seed cases, and it is only then that you see why it is called toothwort: a veritable row of vegetable dentures sticking out of the earth. In bygone days it was thought that God gave each plant a 'signature' that hinted at its usefulness: lungwort for respiratory complaints, woundwort for wounds, and so on. But as far as I know, no dentist has ever tried to calm his struggling patient with essence of toothwort.

As I walk through the wood on a narrow branching track, I realise sadly that the holloway is the best bit, the last stand of the loveliness that was once Love's Copse. Like most of the small woods of the parish, the estate didn't know what to do with it once the demand for hazel fences had ceased by the 1970s. So they chopped most of it down and tried to start again. But the planted larch trees didn't like our chalky clay. Their timber is worthless. The wood is ruled by pheasants now. In two hours, the only other person I meet is a woman walking the other way, from Aldbourne. She likes the flowers too, especially the primroses, and looks forward to returning when the bluebells are out.

Tuesday 7 April

Michael: We're still getting over the shock of Boris Johnson being moved last night to intensive care (he was hospitalised on Sunday after a week with coronavirus and getting no better). A shock it was indeed, because it looked very likely he was going to die. As soon as I heard the news, the old newspaperman in me took over and I logged on to the websites of the *New York Times* and the *Washington Post*: it was leading both papers, as I thought it would, a huge world story. But he survived the night and is said to be stable, so maybe he'll pull through. I hope so. I hope everyone pulls through who gets it, although UK deaths went up today by a record jump of 786 to 6,159. At this rate it'll be a thousand a day by Easter. It couldn't be more horrifying.

At least the weather is a consolation: it was yet another lovely spring day of soft sunshine, and Jo and I walked through Sheen Wood, where I heard my first chiffchaff of the year, and then my first blackcap, to the Bog Gate of Richmond Park and out into the park itself. I aim to traverse the whole place on foot to drink deep of its wildlife; today we walked to the Sheen Gate and back, and saw a sparrowhawk circling and two green woodpeckers feeding close by on the anthills that dot the grassland – not a bad start.

Tonight there was a strikingly bright and fat full moon, a 'supermoon' (when it's at its closest point to the earth of the year). I went out into the garden to gaze up at it at midnight; there was no sound. Normally there would have been a lot of traffic noise, even at that time, from the A316 dual carriageway, the main road into London from the M3; now there was nothing.

Peter: The prime minister is in intensive care! Statistically that means his chances of staying alive are about 50:50. I must admit, that thought gave me a restless night. Quite apart from concern for Boris, such news tends to bring one face to face with one's own mortality. He's younger than me! Fitter too, possibly.

I wander down to the Seven Bridges, where the chiffchaffs have lately been joined by willow warblers. There are several of them, living up to their name by singing from willow thickets. Their descending cadence of sweet, soft whistles is repeated over and over, always the same, as unvarying as the chiffchaff's *chiff* and *chaff*. How the nonsinging female chooses between so many identical songs is a mystery. She presumably teases out subtle variations, comparing each effort for timbre, tuning and sheer loudness. They are singing only a few yards away now, but I still cannot see them. Glimpsing a willow-green bird little larger than a leaf in the middle of a willow thicket requires better eyes than mine. With warblers, I look not so much for a bird as a moving shadow. Sometimes the first thing you spot is the sharp bill, snapping open and shut like a pair of nail scissors.

The willows bear catkins, some robust, upright and prickly-looking, others long and tasselled, like Christmas decorations. Time was when I did my best to identify the trees growing along our lane and across the marsh. We are a very willowy place. I found at least seven different kinds – bushy almond willow, purple willow and osier; the tree-sized ones, crack willow and white willow; plus the nectar-rich sallows, grey sallow and the so-called goat willow. There were also a couple of indeterminate ones that I decided were probably hybrids. Their catkins, all produced in the spring, are good clues to their identity. Purple willow is the earliest and neatest: silky grey catkins bearing bright red stamens that turn yellow when they are ripe, giving a sort of tutti-frutti effect. They look like exotic caterpillars. Fittingly, the biggest patch of purple willow, by the third bridge, is a favourite place for singing birds: marsh tit, reed bunting, and up to four warblers, including our eponymous willow warbler.

The warblers are returning to our valley. They sing as they have always done, from long before the time when our bit of valley became a village. They are utterly unconcerned with our triumphs and tragedies. They sing on, and we call it the sound of spring.

Wednesday 8 April

Michael: Because of the quiet of the lockdown, I have discovered a local colony of house sparrows here in the streets of Richmond, and I am elated. How bizarre such a statement would have seemed thirty years ago and more, when *Passer domesticus* was abundant throughout London, as it was throughout Britain and indeed around the globe: the most widespread and familiar bird in the world. But in the 1990s, something catastrophic happened within the ecosystem of London's sparrows, and in a few short years they disappeared. Take St James's Park in the heart of the capital. In the 1980s, it held sparrows by the hundred, so many that people used to sell birdseed by the end of the bridge over the lake, and you could buy a packet and have twenty birds on your arm within seconds. But the last known pair nested in the park in 1998, and by the millennium, they were all gone.

Nobody knows why. When I was a journalist on the *Independent*, we offered a £5,000 prize for a proper scientific solution to the mystery, and it was never awarded; it's a mystery still. I discussed it extensively with the world expert on sparrows, Denis Summers-Smith, a former ICI engineer who had spent a lifetime studying them. His belief was that air pollution from road traffic was killing off the small insects the chicks needed as food in the first few days of their life, but the theory was never proved. All that was known was that the sparrows were gone, and in a quarter of a century of living in this house, we've never had one in the garden. I didn't think there were any in Richmond or Kew; there are certainly none left in Kew Gardens, where once they flocked for crumbs around the cafés.

Yet today I discovered a small colony of the birds, four streets away. I did so because of the silence – the colony is a stone's throw from the A316, which normally roars with traffic, and it is right under the flight path of Heathrow-bound jets thundering over less than two thousand feet up. But this morning, with no planes and very few cars, my ears picked up the slight abrupt *cheep!* that house sparrows make from deep within a bush or under the eaves, and eventually I glimpsed, to my delight, a couple of birds. Talking to local people, I realised that the colony focuses on a small recreation ground behind the houses, and there at last I glimpsed a small flock of about fifteen birds, a sight I thought I would never see here. That's the lockdown dividend, at the other end of the scale from feasting your eyes on buzzards and red kites.

Peter: A steep, shaded bank on our lane is often covered with liverworts in winter and early spring. I think it is one with the scientific name of *Conocephalum*, and known in English as snakewort, because its deep-green lobes have a scaly look to them, or great scented liverwort because it is supposed to 'smell of stale urine'. Despite its dubious perfume, I like this liverwort because it is so odd and primitive. Liverworts are stripped-down plants that remind you more of seaweed than any other form of life, thick and green, and uncomplicated. The first land plants must have looked like this, a lumpy skin of green clinging to the shore of those bare, ancient lakes. Nothing much has happened in the world of liverworts since the Silurian. They found their niche in life a very long time ago, on moist banks halfway between the wet and the dry, and, quite literally, they stuck to them.

I feel the same way about the horsetails in my flower beds. The common or field horsetail is a most pernicious weed, quite impossible to get rid of short of blitzing the earth with poisons. But it is another age-old survivor, and one of the hardiest plants in the world. The feathery horsetail of our gardens with its grooved, jointed stem, lives equally happily in the high arctic on some of the northernmost ice-free land in the world. Iguanodons once grazed on horsetails in the Sussex marshes, and when we burn coal we are consuming the crushed remains of even more ancient ancestors. Yes, it's a noxious weed, but it's also a little touch of the Carboniferous here at home in Ramsbury.

Jeremy: The death toll in the UK is going up terrifyingly fast – over 900 a day now and rising uncontrollably, it seems. There is palpable fear in the air. Notices have gone up today all around the village, pinned to gates and stiles, warning of the risks of contagion from such surfaces. I've just seen a couple approach a stile, read the notice and recoil as if from an electric shock. The man then tried to mount the stile without using his hands on the supports but got the wobblies and came back down. I could see him even wondering about vaulting over it for a mad moment. I left them searching for some gloves. But how would that help? It's just another skin you'll be touching things with.

It's a reminder of how important our sense of touch is in navigating the world and sensing it, a crucial faculty turned against us as a weapon in these extraordinary circumstances. Ironically, I've been finding a new pleasure in touching leaves this year, comparing the rough felting of the wayfaring tree's leaves, for example, with the softness of the emerging horse chestnut ones, just like floppy little lamb's ears. I wonder how many other trees I could identify in a blind test this way? Holly would be easy, of course, and I'd hope I could work out oak, beech, birch, sycamore, hawthorn, hazel and willow, from a combination of texture, shape and size. Alder, field maple, hornbeam and elm might be initially more challenging but I'm sure could be learned. Memo to self to try sometime.

Most animals depend crucially on touch, and for a whole range of purposes, not just navigation. Think of monkeys grooming each other to promote social bonding, or young foals like the ones in the paddock here nestling against their mothers for comfort and security. It's not just obvious cases like this, though. There are a couple of mallards dabbling in the old ford over the river in Great Thurlow. They can't see much through the muddy water, but I've learned from a fascinating book called *Bird Sense* by Tim Birkhead that the apparently inanimate horny bills of some birds like these mallards are in fact studded with the most sensitive touch receptors that can distinguish immediately between edible and non-edible items in their siftings. The green woodpecker

I saw here this morning on an old oak has a similar capacity, perhaps even more remarkable in this case, since here the bill itself is like a hardened machine-tool and is used for drilling holes in tree trunks; but woodpeckers also have very long tongues, whose super-sensitive sticky tips can distinguish in the same way between larvae and whatever other detritus they touch when they are extended down tree holes. The extraordinary amidst the familiar everywhere in nature.

4

The Easter Weekend and the Cuckoo: 9–14 April

Suburban violets, Gilbert White and Henry David Thoreau, holly blues, the song thrush as a comedian, a willow warbler in a willow tree, a stately home for a nuthatch, the scarlet bottom of a great spotted woodpecker, rainbows moving, frog sex, goldcrests and a lesser whitethroat singing, and the first cuckoo of the spring

Thursday 9 April: Maundy Thursday

Michael: A day of almost dreamlike loveliness on the borders of Richmond and Kew: soft warm air and blue skies, and the quiet streets filled with blossom: the choisya, the wisteria and the ceanothus are now out, decorating the front gardens alongside the later cherries, the ones with the big fat pendulous pink and white blooms. In Ennerdale Road, the green of the new leaves, especially the horse chestnuts, is so iridescent and lustrous that they seem almost blossoms themselves. And meanwhile, 881 more people have died in hospital, I imagine most of them in great distress away from their loved ones. What a conjunction.

But I took hope from something, a sort of urban survivor

that delighted me: wild violets. I've never seen wild violets in the suburbs before, but here they were today in the grounds of a modest nearby housing estate consisting of four small blocks of flats. It is surrounded by parked cars and lawns that at the moment are not being mown, so they are full of what gardeners might call weeds, and looking over them, in a forgotten corner between the end of a block and the low wall to the street, I caught a glimpse of a sumptuous deep purple. I went closer, and realised with a thrill that I was looking at some of the loveliest of our wild flowers, a patch of violets the size of a dining table. They should be in woodlands – what on earth were they doing here amongst the daisies and the dandelions? I knew they were either sweet violets or dog-violets, which look similar but are distinguished by the fragrance of the former, so I picked one and was disappointed in sniffing it: nothing. Maybe it was my nose. But still, they were violets, one way or another, with those five glowing purple petals and their heart-shaped leaves, and at once I was reminded of a poem by Robert Herrick, which I encountered when we did the cavalier poets in school. Who reads Herrick today? There is a first line of his that everybody knows, but I doubt if one person in a thousand knows the next three:

> Gather ye rosebuds while ye may,
> Old Time is still a-flying;
> And this same flower that smiles today
> Tomorrow will be dying.

That's from a poem called 'To the Virgins, to Make Much of Time'. In modern terms, Herrick is a songwriter, and his 'To Violets' poem is slight but pleasing, a seventeenth-century pop song (various people have set it to music, from Benjamin Britten down, although personally I would like to see someone like Mark Knopfler have a go at it):

> Welcome, maids-of-honour!
> You do bring
> In the spring,
> And wait upon her.
>
> She has virgins many,
> Fresh and fair;
> Yet you are
> More sweet than any.
>
> You're the maiden posies,
> And so grac'd
> To be plac'd
> 'Fore damask roses.
>
> Yet, though thus respected,
> By-and-by
> Ye do lie,
> Poor girls, neglected.

Jeremy: I'm walking up to Temple End Farm, but I keep well offroad, trespassing along a hedgerow I've never explored before. Perhaps trespassing laws should be relaxed for the duration of lockdown to help maintain social distancing? This will be my defence, anyway: that the injunctions against public gatherings entail a new 'right to roam'. Worth a try . . . The estate has engineered a natural spectacle here, if only accidentally. They scoured out a deep ditch with some heavy machinery earlier in the winter, chewed up the old set-aside in the process and spread the spoil from the ditch in a ten-metre strip on top. This has now released buried treasure, in a riot of wild flowers – brilliant patches of stitchwort, meadow buttercups, cowslips and dandelions, among an emerging tapestry of dog-violets, ground ivy, shepherd's purse, white comfrey, speedwell, red campions and field horsetails, which I'm sure will be joined in the weeks to come by a succession of other newly liberated volunteers. Let's just hope that this gift of spring growth isn't later destroyed by herbicidal spraying.

I go up the hill (well, we call this a hill in Suffolk) to get a grand view back over the whole area in which I'm walking every day. I don't think I'm a claustrophobe, but I'm certainly an agoraphile and always feel physically lightened by the sense of space up here.

There's another watcher inspecting the landscape, too. A kestrel, hovering intently over the hedgerows I've just left. Gilbert White, the spiritual godfather of all nature diarists, described the bird's characteristic behaviour thus: 'The kestrel or wind-hover has a peculiar mode of hanging in the air in one place, his wings all the time being briskly agitated.' And the novelist Virginia Woolf remarked, in her perceptive essay on White's classic *Natural History of Selborne* (1789), that this was also the description that fitted White himself best. He rarely left his small parish, but he was extraordinarily attentive to it and his genius was to conjure the universal out of the parochial. Similarly, White's American counterpart, Henry David Thoreau (1817–62), said of his own home patch, 'I have travelled a good deal in Concord.' It was their depth of understanding of a single place that provided both men with the creative resources and inspiration for their writing. 'Here I have been these forty years,' added Thoreau in his *Journal*, 'learning the language of these fields that I may better express myself.'

Friday 10 April: Good Friday

Michael: Yet another exquisite day, with cloudless skies and the temperature in the seventies. As Jo and I were sitting in the garden, a holly blue flew in and began nectaring on the flowers of green alkanet (which despite the name are themselves blue, with a white 'eye'). I love blue butterflies – the American poet Robert Frost famously called them 'sky-flakes' and 'flowers that fly' – and we are blessed with seven resident species in Britain, the others being the common blue, the silver-studded blue, the chalkhill blue, the Adonis blue, the small blue and the large blue (this last having been successfully reintroduced to the West Country after becoming extinct in 1979). Each is hugely attractive in its own way; the holly blue is distinguished by being the earliest one on the wing – it overwinters as a chrysalis and can emerge in the last week of March – and also by being the only one you're likely to see in an urban environment, not least because the larval food plants, the holly and the ivy, grow in many gardens in towns. (To find the caterpillar food plants for the others, you generally have to go deep into the countryside.) It's a charmingly pretty butterfly and I pointed out to Jo how the underwings are pure pale silvery blue, which is how you tell it apart from the other blues, most of which have some brown or orange on the underwing.

Holly blues have been very plentiful this year, and that's probably because the population goes in cycles of boom and bust, owing to the actions of parasitic wasps. Professor Jeremy Thomas, our leading butterfly expert, explains it in his book *The Butterflies of Britain and Ireland* (the best book on the subject, with fabulous illustrations by Richard Lewington): 'When the wasp is rare, many caterpillars survive, and the butterfly temporarily achieves high densities, but in a year or two the wasp catches up and becomes so abundant, through breeding on its plentiful host, that the number of butterflies plummets. This in turn precipitates a crash in the wasp population, and so the cycle continues.' Maybe we're in a holly blue boom now, and next year we'll see very few. I hope not. Each is a flash of pleasure on a spring day.

Peter: We have reached Italian and Spanish levels of Covid fatalities. Some people seem astonished that we Brits are being so sensible and, by and large, obedient to the government's guidelines on isolation and social distancing. But it's not that surprising really. It's not that we are particularly slavish by nature, or at least I hope we are not. We're just frightened. It's not about what we know so much as what we don't know about the virus. I'm a post-war baby boomer, a stranger to air-raid sirens and bombs, but now I know what fear means. The Aussies call the virus the boomer remover.

If, as the *Reader's Digest* used to say, laughter is the best medicine, I found it today in an unlikely place: a stand-up act performed on top of a bush by a reed bunting. The odd thing was that the bunting was singing like a robin. Now, the bunting is a handsome enough bird, very much the dignified male with its black head, white collar and drooping Victorian moustache. Normally a short jingly song, a few soft whistles and a trill, is the most you can expect from Mr Bunting by way of a performance. Yet this one seemed to be singing its heart out, like a tin whistle played by an artist on amphetamines.

Of course it wasn't the bunting at all but a robin hidden just behind it. Yet the bunting was silently opening and shutting its beak as though the robin was playing it like a ventriloquist's dummy. Anyway, I laughed out loud and Mr Bunting flew off, plainly miffed. The robin stayed behind for the applause.

The lead comedian among songbirds is surely the song thrush. They were singing all over the village in early March, but have quietened down since as the morning chorus has swelled. But yesterday I heard one near the road bridge that was obviously running through the card: weird shrieks one moment, self-satisfied chuckles the next, as if to say to itself, 'That was a good one! I must remember that one!' Perhaps it sounds funny to us because the song thrush is closer than most birds to the rhythms of human speech, especially in its assertiveness (*Be quick! Be quick!*), its ardent questioning (*Did he do it? Did he do it?*) and even its bare-faced cheek (*You twit! You twit!*). And like some others among us, it will never say it once when it can say it twice, as if trying, as Robert Browning put it, to recapture 'the first fine careless rapture'.

Saturday 11 April

Jeremy: I hardly need to leave the garden today. We have a large willow tree, just beginning to droop heavily with catkins, and there first thing in the morning was a real willow warbler, singing its ever-so-gentle rippling cadence time and again until 10 a.m. Neither he nor I tired of it. Then he ghosted away through the greenery, not to be seen or heard again. Apart from the eponymous coincidence, it was such a delight to have one actually in the garden again. Willow warblers used to breed in this village a few decades ago. We've lived here for nearly forty years and I've kept weekly song-charts of all the commonest songbirds for the whole of that period. The willow warbler used to be the second migrant in, after the chiffchaff and just before the blackcap, but it has become more a northern and western species in Britain and we only get them here as fleeting passage birds, like today's little sprite. Nowadays I no more expect a willow warbler in my willow tree than I do a garden warbler in my garden – you need a shrubbery and a bit of woodland for those. Both birds are in my top ten list of favourite songsters and the rich, energised warbling of the garden warbler is a special favourite. One of the grim realisations now dawning on me is that this may be the first year since I was about ten that I won't hear a garden warbler sing, nor a nightingale, since neither species breeds within walking distance.

Mind you, I think I might settle for that as the price of this precious silence, in which every bird song has so much greater clarity and definition, and therefore significance. Gilbert White, again: 'The language of birds is very ancient, and, like other ancient modes of speech, very elliptical; little is said, but much is meant and understood'.

Peter: Our largest oak tree, on a knoll overlooking a mill leat, measures eight metres in girth. It presents to its earthly admirers a cliff face of rugged bark, corky, deeply fissured, a vision of strength. The tree is hemmed in by its neighbours and only stands out from the hillside above. Indications of great age are the corkscrew lower branches, as if they couldn't make up their minds in which direction to grow. A few dead boughs peep from the still lush foliage; a sign of the natural crown die-back of veteran trees. It has no name and no history. It is, simply, the great oak.

The oak has its own herald. Every spring, around early April, a nuthatch calls from somewhere within its vast depths. Its loud, piercing *hweet, hweet, hweet* greets me today as I approach the tree from the Seven Bridges. I expect it has a nest hole up there; if so, it's a stately home to match any great house in the district, as grand as Ramsbury Manor!

Sunday 12 April: Easter Sunday

Michael: Easter Sunday, and Boris Johnson was discharged from hospital today – *he is risen*, said the wags. We thought that even with the lockdown there would be a lot of people exercising in Richmond Park, so we decided to save our walk for later in the day. On a golden evening, Jo and I hiked up through Sheen Wood and had terrific views of a great spotted woodpecker. We heard it before we saw it; it was high up on a tree and knocking bits of bark off the trunk – *knock! knock! knock!* – to get at the grubs underneath, so involved in what it was doing that it didn't seem to notice us, although we were looking straight up at its scarlet bottom.

When we entered the park through Bog Gate, there in front of us were two of its great attractions, the deer and the veteran oak trees. A group of twenty red deer stags were congregating nearby; two jackdaws were perched on the back of one of them, rummaging for ticks, like African oxpeckers on the back of a rhino. The great old oaks, some of which are more than five hundred years old, were all greening: the intense sunshine of the last week has clearly brought them on apace. We walked out over the large expanse of acid grassland known as The Bog – to our astonishment and pleasure, a skylark was singing above us, just over a mile from our suburban front door – and when we got to the crest of the rising ground, I suddenly understood the effect of the absence of motor vehicle traffic: it was reuniting the landscape.

For at the top of this rise, standing next to Two Storm Wood, you look across a natural valley towards another rise on the far side, topped with an oak wood called Saw Pit Plantation. I was moved at how lovely the rolling landscape was, as if I had never seen it before – and then I realised that in effect I never had. Because what was in the dip between the two woods was the road, from Richmond Gate to Sheen Gate and Roehampton Gate. Normally it holds a steady stream of cars, and when you look across, your eye stops at the vehicles and doesn't sweep forward; the vista is cut in half. But now the road was empty and invisible. So for the first time in my experience, I was looking at this historic, miraculously preserved landscape as a whole. I thought it was wonderful.

Peter: For some time now, painted rainbows have shone from village windows, some arching from little clouds, others with an added confetti of stars or hearts. Someone has thanked the NHS in coloured letters on cut wood, displayed in echelon to form a message along the top of the hedge. Further down the lane, a child has chalked rainbows and hearts right across the road itself. There is so little traffic (and no rain) that this rather risky tribute remains as it was drawn. And today, on an Easter Sunday with no worship, there are painted pebbles – stone eggs in rainbow colours – left on walls, or in a little tray by the gate. They make you smile. They cheer you up.

The other day I was looking at a real rainbow, and from where I was standing it seemed to bury itself in my neighbour's garden, where, no doubt, a pot of gold was waiting to be found. One thinks of rainbows as fairly static things, but they aren't. For a start, this one was moving slowly down the valley behind a curtain of rain. And it also pulsated, bright, then faint, then brighter than ever. It was most luminous in the middle, the orange, yellow and green band. The red in the outer border was fuzzy and seemed to tail off into greyish. The blue and violet bands were better defined but narrower, and try as I might, I couldn't see the seventh colour, indigo, that supposedly lies in between. The grazing sheep and their newborn lambs ignored it, and so did their companion rooks and jackdaws. Rainbows don't concern them.

In the story of Noah's Ark, the 'bow in the cloud' signifies God's covenant between the patriarch and 'every living creature that is with you', forever. The rainbow connecting heaven and earth represents the union of God and man. I am not particularly religious, but today, especially, on Easter Sunday, such symbols seem more than usually potent.

Monday 13 April: Easter Monday

Michael: It was cold – the temperature had fallen ten degrees overnight – but there was floral warmth in the garden in the shape of the marsh marigolds that are in flower in our pond. The first bud opened on 3 April and I observed it with real pleasure; now there are more than a hundred of them, golden and glowing in the shade; you almost feel you could warm your hands in front of them. It's one of my favourite wild flowers. The poet and critic Geoffrey Grigson, who produced an incomparable guide to our flower folklore in *The Englishman's Flora* in 1958, wrote of them: 'Shining, sun-like flowers opening while the world is still cold and colourless, and lasting into May; flowers which illuminate grey moors, black woodland, or the black mud by the roots of alder.' Or a garden pond in the suburbs.

It's a great thing to have a pond. It was there when we arrived, more than twenty-five years ago; all we did to it was make it shallower, to safeguard the children, and plant a few things. It used to be a mind-boggling site for frog sex. In mid March there would be mating orgies; not just pairs coupling with abandon, but threesomes, foursomes, even fivesomes going on – maybe, for after a certain point it became impossible to disentangle the flesh, to separate out the ecstatic bodies and the grasping arms and legs. One year I thought I counted seventy individuals. It was like a swingers' convention in Florida. If you filmed it for a documentary, you'd have to show it after the watershed.

Then one morning about three years ago, I came down to the kitchen at 6 a.m. and looked out of the window into the garden, and to my astonishment, in our pond, which is only the size of a circular dining table, was a heron. It had clearly spotted the glint of the morning sun on the water and come down to see if there was any breakfast going; and there was. I shooed it away, but it was too late. It or its companions have clearly returned, and now we have the odd frog, but no more: the mass orgies are a thing of the past. Pond skaters and aquatic snails are fine, but aren't quite the same.

Jeremy: The day is as chilling as the latest Covid news – well over 10,000 deaths in total now, and that excludes those in care homes, which we are just learning with a shudder have been neglected in the daily rollcall of UK deaths so far; indeed, perhaps neglected altogether, as if they literally 'didn't count'.

Is the lovely spell of sunny weather over already? The butterflies have temporarily disappeared, but there is still plenty of early morning birdsong, stimulated by light rather than temperature. One bird I've heard more often in the village this year than most recent ones is the goldcrest, Britain's smallest bird, only the weight of a 20p coin. There must have been four or five of them singing in the Scots pine plantation today. It's a very high-pitched, needle-sharp song, which has a characteristic pulsating rhythm, as if the bird was inflating its tiny lungs with a pump and then letting its breath out again in a hurried exhalation at the end.

But why so many goldcrests this year? It could be a local population increase, following a succession of mild winters, but I wonder if a contributory reason might be that goldcrest songs can be simply inaudible against the background of the usual plane and road traffic noise – the cocktail party problem, for anyone over the biblical three score years and ten. I remember an article in an ornithological journal a few years ago, suggesting that a reported decline of goldcrests was largely attributable to the advancing age of the loyal band of recorders . . . Worse still, the goldcrests may not even be able to hear *each other* in 'normal' conditions now. There's research to suggest that birds with softer songs are having to abandon otherwise suitable habitats by motorways for just that reason. One bird that doesn't have that problem, however, is the lesser whitethroat I can hear singing over a hundred yards away. It's my first for the year, a couple of days earlier than usual, and its song has a penetrating thudding tempo, usually described as a rattle. I was trying to convey that song to Mike last year, so I'll tell him it's arrived.

Peter: We learn today that coronavirus is hitting a disproportionate number of people of black, Asian and minority ethnic origin, including all ten of the doctors who have died of the virus so far. The BBC news has no explanation to offer. It is a complete mystery. Instead it returns briskly to the nightly briefing, the opinionated experts, the stricken patients, the weeping relatives, and heroic nurses battling on with worn-out masks and one respirator for the four of us.

The sun is still shining, but a cold westerly wind blows down the valley. The warblers are arriving: now the reed warbler, back to its reeds, now the blackcap, whistling sweetly from a tangle of hawthorn. I watch a chiffchaff hopping about on an alder. It never stays still for a second, but drops a phrase or two, forced out from deep in its little breast, then hops on a few steps and sings again. Perhaps it will be heard better there. Its posture is alert, its dark bill pin-sharp. The *chiff* and the *chaff* of its simple see-saw song are snapped out as individual notes with the shortest of pauses between them.

In the past few days they have been joined by the blackcaps. These are usually harder to spot than the chiffchaffs.

I counted six singing birds over about 500 metres of scrub on the three sides of our meadow, but have so far only managed to spot one of them. Blackcaps are not particularly shy – they sing unconcernedly within a few yards of the viewer, occasionally even popping out to take a look at you. But they do like to sing from cover, among a mess of baby leaves, and they take long bounds from twig to twig between snatches of song. Fortunately they are heavier than the chiffchaff. When a blackcap bounds, the twig quivers. You see the movement, though you often miss the bird. Or if you do glimpse its black-capped head with its raised crest of feathers, something else promptly distracts you, and by the time you return, the blackcap has gone.

I love the blackcaps' song, which they keep up far into summer. It becomes one of the sounds of the village in April and May, for they sing everywhere, even in gardens. From a distance you hear only the sweet whistling, but close up you get the grace notes, the subtle gurgles and chuckles. It is a happy song, but tread unwittingly close to a nest and you hear something quite different, a loud double *chack*, like two pebbles banged together. You don't need a course in birdsong to know what it means. It says: I am angry. You go away. And if you don't, I'm going to *chack* a second time!

Tuesday 14 April

Peter. The first cuckoo! It is early this year. Last year I heard it for the first time on 21 April. For the past ten years I have never known it sing this early. Perhaps the recent warm weather has quickened its desire to be here, back in the Kennet valley among the willow bushes, the knee-high sedge, the patches of reed, and the well-hidden nests of its likely victim, the reed warbler. Spring may be here already, by the reckoning of the sun and the greening spray all around, but for those of us lucky enough to have a cuckoo, it starts right now. Summer is a-coming in. As the old song reminds us, 'he brings us glad tidings, and tells us no lies' (but does the cuckoo really suck the sweet flowers to make his voice clear? Not according to the scientists).

A passer-by on the path to Littlecote spotted my binoc-ulars and cried, excitedly, 'Have you heard it?' Perhaps she is as relieved as I am. Cuckoos are in steep decline in England: the bird is deserting more and more places, and one reason might be a shortage of the hairy caterpillars they like. Hence waiting for our cuckoo is always an anxious time. For this bird is more than just another migrant: it is the actual voice of spring, the season summarised in just two notes, which form a precise musical interval, a descending minor third, usually in the key of D major. Thus it's the bird call that most approximates to human speech – though you can only get it exactly right by whis-tling through your thumbs (which I can't do).

There's something else about it too, perhaps a conjunc-tion of the time, the place and the sunshine that goes straight to our hearts. As dear old Edmundo Ros sang on *Children's Favourites*, 'When it's cuckoo time, it's time to fall in love.'

I wonder: if we saw the cuckoo as a physical presence more often than we do, stretching its long form on the bird table, say, or scything over the lawn on its narrow wings, would it retain the same resonance, the same mystery? I suspect not. Surely it's the disembodied nature of its call that makes it so magical. As Wordsworth expressed it, it's less a bird than a 'wandering voice'. 'From hill to hill it seems to pass / At once far off and near.'

Today's cuckoo was no exception. I first heard it from about three hundred yards away. It was singing from somewhere behind a screen of willows close to the ruins of the Roman villa at Littlecote. Close up, the song has a deeper timbre, a noticeable vibrato, as if the bird is singing from the bottom of a well. Perhaps the 'voice' comes from deep inside the bird's throat, echoing slightly as it escapes from its open bill. It lends the simple call a thrilling emphasis, which the cuckoo then employs as a trick, calling this way and that, loud, then faint, and back again.

I hear this dematerialised voice in Delius's tone poem, *On Hearing the First Cuckoo in Spring*. The sense is of a bird calling from the depths of the countryside. For a while you hear nothing but the rural quiet, the same sense of peace you feel when out in the open air on the first warm days of spring. When you do hear the cuckoo call, from a single oboe in the depths of the orchestra, it takes you by surprise. It feels less like a physical presence than a simple musical counterpoint, a repeated two-note refrain that completes the vision. It's the same with the cuckoo in Respighi's *The Birds*: a bird calling from behind a screen of leaves, heard but not seen.

My immediate feeling on hearing our first cuckoo is one of relief, followed by gratitude. The cuckoo might be a symbol of faithlessness, the cuckold, but this particular cuckoo has been faithful to Ramsbury. I listen enraptured. I don't want to leave, and in the end it is the cuckoo that leaves me, silently winging back up the valley towards the village. 'Merrily sung, cuckoo' goes one of the oldest songs in the language. 'Well you sing, cuckoo. Don't you ever stop now.' *Sumer is icumen in. Lhude sing cuccu. Sing cuccu nu.*

5

The Coming of the Swallows: 15–20 April

Swallow arrival, the Thames towpath, the elusive gropper, an owl madrigal, celandines lesser and greater, a farmed landscape in decay, an egg-laying brimstone, the twizzle, the streedle and the chuggle, herb-paris, moth names, a dead mole and its epitaph, and another swallow (this one just passing through)

Wednesday 15 April

Jeremy: Grass starts growing again at about 10°C (50°F) and you can track the movement of that isotherm across Europe from the Mediterranean to the Arctic, a green wave travelling north at about fifty kilometres a day, bringing with it a new season of light, warmth and growth – and a feeling of abundance and renewal. Surfing that green wave are our migrant birds, and none bears a greater freight of these associations than the swallow, arriving here in mid April from southern Africa. I eagerly expect them at the same time and the same place in our village every year – around Great Thurlow church and barns on 15 or 16 April. And here they are today, bang on schedule. A shot of pure adrenaline. I feel I should be the town crier, announcing as if on a loud airport tannoy, 'The 15 April swallows from

Cape Town have just touched down at Great Thurlow church.' Except that they haven't touched down at all. They are swooping, looping, diving and darting – now close enough for me to see the steely blue sheen on the back and the blood-red face and throat, now banking away again at speed with perfect feather-tip control from those swept-back wings and the long tail streamers. The poet Andrew Young: 'The swallows twisting here and there / Round unseen corners in the air.'

The swallow has long been celebrated as the definitive sign of spring. There they are on the Minoan 'spring fresco' from Santorini, among the very first – and wonderfully evocative – pieces of European art, dated to about 1650 BC. They are there in some of our earliest literature, too: 'Famed herald of sweet-scented spring / Blue swallow', sang the poet Simonides in the sixth century BC. And they were special favourites of Gilbert White, who looked out for them longingly every year and greeted his first returning birds on 13 April 1768 with the short, ecstatic diary note '*Hirundo domestica*!!!' (his triple exclamation marks).

Nowadays we await them no less eagerly, but perhaps more anxiously. We think of them as returning home to our English landscapes; but is southern Africa, where they spend our winter, also home? These same swallows were swooping over elephants and ostriches not so long ago. As the world's climate heats and the journey back over barriers like the fast-expanding Sahara desert become ever more arduous, suppose the benefits of long-distance migra-tion no longer prove worth the physical risks and effort for some species. Perhaps the swallows might never come at all one year? Or suppose they were to stay? Chiffchaffs and blackcaps are already doing so regularly in our milder winters now. And if we had swallows at Christmas, what would that do to our emotional responses – to swallows, spring and the seasons? The world is disturbed in more ways than one at present.

Michael: More Covid bad news today: it appears that as many as 4,000 people may have died in care homes, which is not reflected in the official death figures – they only refer to hospitals. I talked about it to Jo and she said it was perfectly possible (she's involved in it all). Jesus. To take our minds off it, this evening we walked the Thames towpath from Richmond to Kew. It follows the Surrey bank and is naturally divided into two halves: the first half, alongside a wooded overgrown flood relief channel called the Mini Ha-Ha, is virtually a green tunnel; later it becomes much more open. While we were in the tunnel, a figure on a bike wearing a red bandanna over his face in lieu of a medical mask shot past us and came to a screeching halt; I thought for a split second it was a cycling highwayman and we were being held up. But it turned out to be Franko the birder, with news; he said that from his roof ('the Richmond bird observatory') he was watching red kites every day over the Royal Botanic Gardens and thought they might be prospecting to nest. Red kites nesting in London once more; that would be quite something . . .

Of course, the absence of planes might make it possible this year, for the other westbound flight path into Heathrow – the northern one, a mile away from the southern one above our house – tracks right over the middle of the gardens. It goes from the main entrance down to the river and then over Syon Park on the opposite bank, the historic estate with its great house and its park designed by Capability

Brown. On a day of spring or summer sunshine the planes can completely shatter the peace of Kew and break its floral spell, but when we stopped to rest opposite Syon, there was nothing in the air but gnats. In the evening sunlight the river was serene; the waterfowl, including a great crested grebe, were letting themselves be carried upstream on the incoming tide. The absence of jumbo jets with their wheels down roaring over this exact spot barely 1,500 feet overhead made the peace incomparable. The lockdown meant that even the distant growl of the M4 was stilled. The sun was sinking behind Syon Park and backlighting the willows on the far bank, the only piece of natural riverbank left on the tidal Thames, still exactly the way it was when Gloriana, the first Queen Elizabeth, was rowed upstream past it to her favourite palace at Richmond. I said to Jo: 'Drink it all in, because it will never be this beautiful again.'

Thursday 16 April

Peter: The gropper is back. We only ever get one a year, and here it is again, an eerie, penetrating voice from deep in the marsh. The gropper is a grasshopper warbler, our most elusive, and, in some ways, our strangest warbler. It has only one song, a long, high-pitched trill often described as a reel, because it sounds a bit like the wind of a fishing reel. It is also, of course, why this is the grasshopper warbler, though no British grasshopper makes a noise quite like that, and definitely not in the spring. If you hear what sounds like the granddaddy of all grasshoppers from the depths of the marsh, you have a gropper.

I wish I could watch it sing. On film you see the perched bird with its bill wide open, tensed and making this extraordinary sound through its puffed-up throat. But all I've seen of ours is the odd glimpse of a little dark bird disappearing into the sedge. Part of the trouble is that you can't pin it down. By constantly turning its head this way and that, the gropper can throw its voice, sending forth its trill in all directions like a sonic beam, and so giving the impression of being in several places at once. The impression is that of a rotating microphone. I'm grateful I can still hear it. A sign of age-related deafness is when you can no longer detect a gropper (or a gold-crest, or a treecreeper).

But even such remote, sonorous contacts are a matter of luck. At first the gropper sings by day, maybe all day. Then you may not hear it for days on end, and you think, we've lost the gropper; it has moved on, perhaps to a bigger, better marsh downriver. And then, to your surprise and relief, you hear it again, as you cross the Seven Bridges on a quiet, warm evening to listen to the chorus of warblers. We only ever seem to have one singing bird, presumably one of a pair, but it is faithful to us; it creeps into the marsh unseen, like the tiny brown mouse it resembles, and all we know of its presence is this long, loud, disembodied reel, the song of the marsh on a fine spring evening.

One year, at the annual Birdfair held by Rutland Water, I bought a life-sized wooden model of a gropper, bill open, throat a-popping, reeling from its twig. It sits in the window overlooking the habitat where the real one might be calling. To me, it is the spirit of the place, all the more potent for hardly ever being seen.

Jeremy: I heard a tawny owl the other night along the Temple End Road, ululating its quavering *oo-oo-oooo.*

Compare the traditional transcription in the madrigal by the seventeenth-century composer Thomas Vautor, 'Sweet Suffolk Owl', which begins:

> Sweet Suffolk owl, so trimly dight
> With feathers, like a lady bright;
> Thou sing'st alone, sitting by night,
> 'To whit! To whoo!'

These lines sing better than they read, but even in Vautnor's rendering, it's usually the male that sings 'To whoo' and the female that answers 'To whit'. Never mind, in truth we all see and hear what we want to with owls. With the possible exception of penguins, they are the most easily humanised of all birds. The combination of the upright stance on two legs, the soft tubby body shape, large head, flat face, big round eyes and steady gaze make them perfect material for the soft toys department. Add their magical ability to see in the dark, their other-worldly cries and ghostly flight, and you can see what a perfect receptacle they are into which to project a whole range of human emotions. They have accordingly featured in fables from Aesop onwards and provide such favourite characters in children's stories as Old Brown in Beatrix Potter, the (dyslexic) Wol in A. A. Milne, and Wise Owl in Alison Uttley. But they also play darker roles in myth and legend: 'an abomination' according to the Bible, Shakespeare's 'fatal bellman' in *Macbeth*, and 'birds of omen dark and foul' for Sir Walter Scott.

Owls are neither wise nor ominous by constitution, however. They are just superbly equipped predators, with some special biological adaptations that have accidentally given rise to these cultural perceptions. Those flat faces are really large facial discs shaped to funnel to their super-sensitive ears the faintest sounds made by invisible scurrying rodents. A tawny owl also has an exceptional spatial memory to enable it to navigate through familiar woodlands in almost pitch darkness; and to help further with night vision, their eyes are so large that they occupy all the space in their sockets – they can't therefore swivel their eyes but can compensate by rotating their heads up to 270 degrees. Their flight feathers have special baffles at the forward edge to muffle the sound of their wings and give them the advantage of surprise. And so on, every detail serving a purpose. The precision and efficacy of these adaptations is astonishing – and quite reason enough to inspire wonder, dread . . . or even a madrigal.

Friday 17 April

Michael: The celandines, the lesser and the greater, are our swallow flowers; they're named from the Greek word for swallow, *chelidon*, because they are signs of spring just as the bird is. The lesser celandine is ubiquitous in March, with its eight golden petals low on the ground; it always gives my spirits a boost when I see the first, because it means the winter is nearly done. The greater celandine, which stands upright with yellow flowers of four petals, is much less familiar, so it was something of a botanical treat when I encountered a patch of it today in the lane that runs up between the Royal Botanic Gardens and the London Welsh rugby ground. I had wandered up there out of hunger to glimpse the Kew bluebells, which will be just coming out now. I was peering into the gardens, but the lane only takes you so far and stops short of the bluebell wood; bluebells saw I none, alas.

But I was reminded of a famous confusion, because the greater swallow flower, *Chelidonium majus*, which I was admiring, is not related to the lesser, *Ficaria verna*. The first is in the poppy family; the latter is in the buttercups, and it was the favourite flower of Wordsworth: he wrote three lesser celandine poems, and only one about daffodils, although the latter has ended up his best-known poem of all. After his death in 1850, a marble memorial to him in St Oswald's church, Grasmere, was commissioned from the young Pre-Raphaelite sculptor Thomas Woolner; at the base, on either side of a striking relief of the poet's head, Woolner carved four of his best-loved flowers, the daffodil, the violet, the snowdrop and the celandine. But which celandine is it?

Many people who have examined it say it's the wrong one. I have not seen the memorial personally, but squinting hard at the photo, it looks like a greater celandine to me. Grasmere is the prettiest place, if somewhat swamped by tourists; the next time I'm there, I will have a look in person.

Peter. The morning rose cool and cloudy, and now it is raining. The blackcap on the far side of the lane continues to sing, gallantly, unstoppably, but otherwise the sound is of water dripping from the gutter and splashing the path. My view, turned into grisaille by the dark clouds, is of a field scored with the lines of defunct drains, and beyond it the far side of the valley where the slope climbs to the local wood, Whitehill Coppice.

The meadow is owned by a neighbour. It is currently

'shut up' (that is, the livestock has been removed). The field will be shorn for a crop of hay in July, and then, after a short interval while the grass recovers, the sheep will be reintroduced. Newborn lambs were bouncing there last month. Haymaking and after-grazing are the traditional uses of a meadow, year on year, and this portion of my view might have been familiar to the original inhabitants of my cottage two centuries ago.

But the rest is all change. The patch of former down has been reseeded; the wood battered by various half-cock replantings (and ravaged by too many deer). The hedgerow elms have gone and the ash trees are dying. In some ways the view is probably wilder than before. The old farm system used our meadows, downs and woods quite intensively. Back then my view would have been of a much neater, interlinked system, busy with woodmen, labourers, shepherds, and the man who looked after the field drains, known as a drowner. On the drier land further west, barley was grown. It still is. The brewers claim that Ramsbury's barley is the best in the world. The proof lies in the local beer, Ramsbury Gold.

A farmed landscape in decay can support a lot of wildlife. So can our scrubbed-up downs, our pheasant-clogged woods, and the river that no longer flows clear and deep. When the sun is out, the view seems to smile at you. But under dull skies, you see it for what it is – and for what we are. It is a ruin, patched up by city money. Mankind is an agent of change. We cannot help it. Wherever we go, whatever we do, we recreate the environment in our own fashion. Most wildlife, on the other hand, prefers things to stay as they are. That is one reason why progress and conservation are in permanent collision, and always will be. Ramsbury is still green. But it is the green of city banknotes as much as of the spring grass.

Saturday 18 April

Michael: It was a sublime, cloudless day. Jo and I were in the garden eating our mushroom salad lunch when I said to her: 'Look.'

'What?'

I pointed. 'Look.'

A large butterfly, pure white, had flown in, and was fluttering around one of the alder buckthorn bushes I planted last year in the hope of attracting brimstones.

Jo said: 'What is it?'

I said: 'It's a female brimstone. She's found it. She's found the alder buckthorn.'

She said: 'You mean . . . it's going to lay eggs?'

I said: 'Well let's see.'

We watched, captivated. All snowy elegance, she flitted and hovered, this brimstone, as if uncertain, then landed on a leaf. I said: 'She can smell it through her feet.' She took off, before coming back and landing on another leaf; she stayed for a while, then repeated the process several times.

Jo said: 'Is it egg-laying?'

I said: 'I hope so, but I dunno.'

When she eventually flew away, we went over to the bush and examined the leaves. I could see nothing and felt a keen disappointment. But Jo said: 'Look at the undersides.' And there, to my intense delight, I spotted half a dozen yellow pinheads.

I used to think that having your own swallows – I mean

swallows nesting in the place where you live – was almost the greatest gift life could bestow upon you. But having your own brimstones is also pretty good; these exquisite insects, the flashing yellow male and that lovely female, which is actually the very faintest pale green but appears a silky white from any distance. If parasitic wasps or blue tits don't get them, the caterpillars will pupate and hatch out in late summer, in the second half of July, and then they will nectar on our buddleia bushes, which will be in full bloom. They will be lemon yellow and pale green, perching on royal-purple flower spikes. I couldn't believe how blessed we were.

Peter. At last I see a swallow. It is late this year, or more likely, I am late in seeing it. A single bird, it flits silently, with that familiar fluid motion, across my sight line and out over the field towards the river. Later on, I hear the distinctive chitter of another, and spot it flying low over the churchyard. One swallow does not make a summer, and neither do two, yet we have been enjoying warm summer weather for some time now. Where have they been?

The answer, probably, is that they have been here all the time, for a week at least, but perhaps flying high, or keeping to certain points in the valley where there are plenty of insects. Normally I hear the scratchy twitter of the first swallow before I see it. Last year, on the same date as this, I looked up from my weeding to spot Swallow One calling from my TV aerial. My earliest was in 2012, on 28 March, sitting on an overhead wire by the canal. Two years before that, on 18 April, a pair were investigating the nesting possibilities of a nearby car port. But the wide scatter of my first dates over the past decade says more about my defects as a birdwatcher than it does about the habits of swallows. Others in the village, especially Eddie, the river keeper, always see them before I do.

I haven't yet spotted a house martin. About now I sometimes saw them in a large flock, looking from a distance like a swarm of bees, hawking gnats above the river marshes. By the end of the month, they disperse to their usual nesting sites, a few in the village, but annoyingly, far more in the next village. My term for the martin's call is a twizzle. On close-up recordings, it sounds more whistly, but heard from a distance, there's an explosive 'z' in there, at least to my ear. My name for the dunnock's song, in case you're interested, is a streedle. It helps me differentiate it from that of a robin. And I hadn't really thought about it until now, but I suppose a reed warbler's is a chuggle.

Sunday 19 April

Jeremy: I did a moth trapping overnight, my first this year. Come the morning, the moths will usually be hiding immobile in the egg boxes you've placed inside the light-box to which they've been attracted. You then gently shake them out onto nearby bushes and they instantly disappear without trace, like a wondrous dream fading on waking. Magic.

The intriguing title of Michael McCarthy's book *The Moth Snowstorm* refers to the phenomenon familiar from a few decades back whereby you'd see a veritable blizzard of moths in your car headlights (messily transferred onto your windscreen). Not now, since there has been a catastrophic decline in moth numbers in the last fifty years. Most people would be surprised, however, by the number of different species you can still find in your own garden. They might be even more surprised by their wonderful names. Who could fail to be entranced to know that we have living amongst us such creatures as the flounced rustic, pebble prominent, frosted orange, willow beauty, true lovers' knot, powdered Quaker, dingy footman, tawny shears and Hebrew character? I had this last in my trap overnight. It's so called from the mark on its wing resembling the character *nun* in the Hebrew alphabet. ‏נ‎. I also had another moth whose name goes one better, the setaceous Hebrew character. Try rolling that around on your tongue. 'Setaceous' means 'bearing a bristle' and it refers to the white line round the *nun* mark on the wing. The scientific names of moths are just as extraordinary as the English ones. How about *Amphipyra tragopoginis* 'fire-flier with a goat's beard' (the mouse moth) or *Lacanobia thassalina* 'sea-green vegetable eater' (the pale-shouldered brocade)?

How I love these names − you can have a pretty good evening just reading the index of a moth fieldguide! It will be a disaster for the planet if insect numbers (including those of moths and butterflies) continue to decline so precipitously, since insects are at the base of the food chain on which everything else depends; but it will be a spiritual tragedy if we risk losing, along with the moths, this treasury of the most extraordinary and beautiful names given to any animal group.

Peter. With the sun peeping coyly from behind a cloud, I set out on the long walk past the manor towards Axford. A friend in the village has found an unusual plant that she thinks is herb-paris. Using her directions, I find a way in to a scrubby strip of ash woodland by an arm of the river, and there it is: a big patch of this weird lily, about two hundred plants in fresh flower, each one a kind of coronet of yellow borne on a cushion of green. Below the solitary flower are four broad leaves positioned like the points of a compass. This neat arrangement of leaves and flowers supplies the plant's name, paris, from the Latin *pars*, which means 'of equal', a reference to the equal-sized, orderly leaves. And it is a herb because (presumably when it was commoner than now) it was considered useful in medicine. Among other things, its single black poisonous berry guarded against epilepsy and witchcraft.

You wonder how long it has been there, in this one corner of Ramsbury's many small woods and, as far as I know, no other. There is a wood in Northumberland where it was recorded nearly five hundred years ago, in one of the first precise records of any British plant. The wood is still there, and herb-paris still grows in it, perhaps even on the same spot. Knowing that, you wonder how long it has been *here*, flowering unseen. Perhaps it can remember the times when there were beavers on the river, or the distant days when Ramsbury was an important place, with more corn mills than Newbury and Swindon combined, with fifty-four plough teams, and its own bishop (long since removed to Salisbury). Long may it thrive in this secret place!

Monday 20 April

Jeremy: Right on the footpath there's a mole. A dead one, I'm afraid. I think it must have been caught by a fox and discarded here, since I can see it's been bitten and we're a little way from the meadows by the river, where I often see mole diggings (but almost never the diggers). I'm always surprised how small moles look close-up, compared to the scale of their underground excavations. This one can't be more than 15 cm long: a short, stocky body with powerful shoulders and those large, nakedly white front feet shaped like rounded shovels, which is exactly their function. The Middle English name for moles was *moldwarp* or 'earth throwers', and so they do. They can almost swim through the earth, in a kind of breaststroke action. If you disturb one on their rare visits to the surface, they can dive and disappear astonishingly fast; and when at work mining, it's been calculated that in twenty minutes a single hundred-gram mole can shift a phenomenal six kilos of soil, the equivalent of a medium-sized man moving four tons. They are voracious eaters, but surprisingly fussy in handling the worms that are their principal prey. They usually bite off their tails, paralysing them with a toxin, then turn them around, taking their heads in their mouths to squeeze the earth out from the tail end before storing them, still alive, to eat at their leisure.

Most people know moles best for their soft velvety fur. When William of Orange died from injuries suffered when he was thrown from his horse, which had stumbled on a molehill, the Jacobites were said to have raised their glasses to 'the little gentleman in black velvet'. Taupe is the usual description of the colour now (from the French word for a mole, *taupe*); and if you rub your finger over its fur, as I've just done, rather hesitantly, you can feel its dense texture, which unlike most animal fur has no one direction to the nap.

When you see a little mole corpse stranded on the ground like this, you realise what an upside-down world they live in, aptly expressed by the Scots-born Andrew Young (1885–1971), who was a clergyman as well as a poet:

> Strong-shouldered mole,
> That so much lived below the ground,
> Dug, fought and loved, hunted and fed,
> For you to raise a mound
> Was as for us to make a hole;
> What wonder now that being dead
> Your body lies here stout and square
> Buried within the blue vault of air?

I conducted a burial in a shallow grave to return him to his own element. The words of the common Roman funerary inscription seemed the appropriate ones: *Sit tibi terra levis* – 'May the earth sit lightly on you'. The reverse injunction to humankind, that we tread lightly on the earth, seems ever more important in these times.

Michael: I have been thinking again during the last week about what I will miss this year through the lockdown, besides the Kew bluebells: orchids, especially burnt, fragrant, greater butterfly and pyramidal; spring butterflies you can't find in the suburbs, such as the green hairstreak; and among birds, the willow warbler for its song, the cuckoo, of course, and the swallow for – well, for everything about it. No swallows swooping in my road with heart-stopping aerial elegance; no swallows in Richmond at all that I know of, although there is a road in Kew with house martins. But this evening the swallow situation changed, if only for an ephemeral moment. Jo and I were returning from our walk to Richmond Park, and just as we had strolled over the

level crossing at North Sheen station, she exclaimed, 'Isn't
that a swallow?' I looked up and cried out, 'It bloody is
an' all!' We watched the bird flying strongly for five or six
seconds before it disappeared, a passage migrant, heading
north-east over the allotments to – where? Norfolk?
Yorkshire? Aberdeen? Orkney? Wherever, as a site-faithful
bird, as they all are, it knew where it was going, and even
though the glimpse of it was fleeting, it was enough for
me to punch the air, and then start chanting Swinburne's
'Itylus' to myself:

> Swallow, my sister, O sister swallow,
> How can thine heart be full of the spring?
> A thousand summers are over and dead.
> What hast thou found in the spring to follow?
> What hast thou found in thine heart to sing?
> What wilt thou do when the summer is shed . . .

6

Bluebell Time: 21–27 April

Bluebells at their peak, different shades of green, dazzling little egrets, the mayfly and its hatches, a wheatear in the suburbs, the black poplar, the St Mark's fly, yellow wagtails, a trio of cuckoos, a tunnel decorated in white flowers, and lords-and-ladies with their perilous berries

Tuesday 21 April

Peter. I walk across the wartime airfield to Burnt Wood to see the bluebells. They are at their peak now, a haze of blue beneath the boughs of hazel and the overarching ash trees. The bluebell has been voted our most popular wild flower, and no wonder: no other country has bluebell woods like ours. As chance has it, Britain has the perfect climate for a flower that is rather finicky: plenty of gentle rain, not too cold in winter, nor too hot and dry in summer, and plenty of small woods that were traditionally managed as coppice, letting in the sunshine and allowing flowers like bluebells to shimmer and sparkle in the dappled light. Nearly all of Ramsbury's natural woods are bluebell woods. They sit on gently sloping chalky clay in which water can run through the bulbs without ponding up and rotting them. And, usefully, almost nothing eats bluebells or digs them up. I'm told muntjac will try them, the way they try anything, but if so, they haven't made any impression on these. The brief blueing of Burnt Wood is simply glorious.

One of the wonders of bluebells is the tricks they play with light. In the light of mid morning, they lose their individuality and shimmer as a wash of colour, a blue mist hanging over the greenery. And yet it isn't quite blue either. In the shade, the flowers form a shadowy grey-purple blur; in sunlight they are a pale purplish blue. At this point it is customary to quote Gerard Manley Hopkins and his 'brakes wash wet like lakes'. It is a wet blue, I'll give him that. It reflects light like water coolly disturbed by a breeze.

The fragrance wafts towards me in waves. It is hard to describe: sweet, delicate, cool and refreshing, somehow sappy. You try to breathe it in and then lose it. It is mildly intoxicating. Bangor University once tried to capture and analyse the scent of bluebells. It turned out to be amazingly complicated, composed of oils called geraniol, citronella and zingiberene, a dozen or more different scents blended with the most extraordinary subtlety. Manufacturing blue-bell scent is virtually impossible. It wouldn't work anyway. It belongs to the woods, with their green shade, their dampness, their otherness.

Returning, I notice that someone, probably a child, has picked a bunch of bluebells and then dropped them in the road, one by one. Traffic has reduced them to a paint-like violet smear. I expect he or she was disappointed with how bluebells look away from their natural setting. They lose their animation and become leggy, drooping, lifeless. To quote Hopkins again, 'Let them be left, O let them be left, wildness and wet'.

Jeremy: I take the ridge path today, leading to Great Wratting. In the double-hedgerow here the hawthorn blossom has now taken over completely from the 'blackthorn winter' I wrote about on 24 March, bringing forward the sweetly scented 'may' well into April. The ground is iron hard after this long dry spell, winter's ruts concreted into ankle-twisters and preserving in some bare clay patches the imprint of deer slots like some prehistoric archaeological record. The new vegetation is growing apace everywhere nonetheless and I head on into a small wood. Battling through the undergrowth on a little-used track I divert myself by imagining some of the more aggressive plants as competing US football teams: the Cleveland Cleavers vs the Houston Hogweeds, in a play-off perhaps to meet the winner of the Nashville Nettles vs the Tallahassee Thistles . . . But in truth all this surging growth and greenery everywhere is wonderfully life-enhancing, whatever its occasional discomforts.

'Greenery', what a lovely word that is. Coleridge seems to have been the first to coin it, in *Kubla Khan* – 'And here were forests ancient as the hills / Enfolding sunny spots of greenery' – but countless poets have invoked the symbolic power of the colour, from Chaucer (in The Squire's Tale) talking of the 'yonge green' of April, through to Dylan Thomas's 'The force that through the green fuse drives the flower / Drives my green age'.

Curiously though, English seems quite impoverished in the adjectives we have to distinguish between different kinds of green. We have emerald, lime, aquamarine, turquoise, lovat, glaucous and perhaps a few more; but to expand the range we are quickly driven to hyphenated comparisons like pea-green, bottle-green, olive-green and apple-green. Why stop at apple and olive trees, though? Keats talks of 'beechen green' in his 'Ode to a Nightingale', but what about holly, willow, oak, sycamore, alder, elm and field maple, to name just a few other, and very different, greens all coming into fresh leaf here now? Then there are all the differences in our perceptions of leaf colour resulting from variations in sheen, opacity and texture. I would have thought some astute naturalist might have seen the potential for some consultancy work here, for example on a more sophisticated Farrow & Ball colour chart?

All very well to sing of 'England's green and pleasant land', but look more closely at it. There is much less of it to celebrate than in Blake's time, and of what remains there are surely at least fifty shades of green for sensuous exploration.

Wednesday 22 April

Michael: I am thinking more and more about the Kew bluebells of 2020, which will be at their very best this week, wondrous in their beauty, and which, in common with the rest of the public, I shall never see. A few days ago, I emailed the Kew director, Richard Deverell, whom I know quite well, having worked on a few projects for him, suggesting that the Royal Botanic Gardens should make a video or photographic record of this great floral climax to the spring. He replied: 'I'm under lockdown but I actually live at Kew so I have the extraordinary privilege of wandering the gardens daily. It's surreal – they are so beautiful, with this glorious weather, yet totally empty.' He went on: 'Yes – the bluebells are just emerging – and they look stunning. I will see if we can get some filming done this week.' The gardens were very tranquil, he said. 'The absence of flights makes a huge difference.'

Richard is an interesting figure, the seventeenth director of the RBG since William Aiton, the first, took up the reins in 1759, and the only non-botanist in the list – he was a senior BBC executive, although he has a natural sciences degree from Cambridge. But he has been a consummate director since taking over in 2012, restoring Kew's finances and presiding over a series of *grands projets* in the French sense, including the renovation of the 1762 Pagoda, the restoration of the Victorian Temperate House – surely now the world's loveliest glasshouse – and the establishment of the new Children's Garden. He has also opened up part of the bluebell wood that was previously out of bounds to the public, by running a wooden boardwalk through it. But he can't get round the coronavirus, new deaths from which were up 759 today to 18,100 – which puts my regret at missing the bluebells into some sort of proper perspective. It's still a pang, though. I can't help it.

Jeremy: I'm peering through the curtain of greenery that now hangs over the riverbank when I glimpse the unmistakable white plumage of a little egret, picking its way along a shallow stretch of water. It has a *dazzling* whiteness, whiter than any detergent advertisement would dare pretend, and far more brilliant than that of a swan or gull. As the egret wades closer, I can also see its contrasting black legs and cute little yellow feet, which it lifts in a deliberate high-stepping gait. Little egrets are quite unusual here, though of course common in much of the southern half of Britain these days. You can't walk anywhere on a Suffolk seawall, for example, without seeing one in a creek or on the marsh. I guess this one must be a non-breeding bird that followed the River Stour up from its mouth to get here.

The Stour, one of several by that name in England (etymology uncertain but probably signifying 'strong'), rises as a spring a few miles away, quickly becomes a stream, and by the time it reaches the Thurlows is already a proper river. From here, it flows through picturesque Suffolk villages like Clare, Cavendish and Long Melford, then on through 'Constable country', forming the border between Suffolk and Essex for much of its length, until it issues finally into the North Sea opposite Harwich, by which time it's almost a mile wide and tidal. My wife Diane and I walked the length of it for our honeymoon, and it's rich in wildlife, history and beauty.

It's hard to remember now just how recently little egrets became such a familiar part of our landscapes. Up to the latter half of the twentieth century this was basic-ally a Mediterranean species, but with global warming they started moving northwards through Europe, and the first pair nested in Britain in 1996 on Brownsea Island in Dorset. Egrets have a longer and deeper symbolic importance in the history of conservation, however. Over a century ago, it was the mass slaughter of egrets to supply fine plumes for ladies' hats that led a group of pioneering female conservationists to found, in 1889 at Didsbury in Manchester, the society that went on to become the modern RSPB. That organisation now has over one million members, more than the members of all our political parties put together. Perhaps the latter need some potent new symbols to highlight the kinds of destruction we currently face a hundred years on? It's officially Earth Day today, so the iconic *Earthrise* photo of 1968 – our first ever sight of the earth from a distance – might be one candidate.

Thursday 23 April

Peter. From the road bridge you can watch the trout, facing upstream as always, keeping station with lazy flicks of their tails. There are at least a dozen today, plump and speckled, waiting patiently for someone to throw down some bread (it's intended for the ducks, not the fish, but the trout often get there first, rippling the water as they rush for the morsel). Come winter, some of them will spawn and lay here, in troughs of fine gravel between the stones called redds. A line of barbed wire suspended from posts has been laid across the water to make life difficult for poachers intent on a bit of free fishing from the bridge.

Our river is a chalk stream. It is fed by an underground aquifer of cold, clear water, purified after passing through a thick layer of chalk. As we wild swimmers know only too well, the water is cold all year round, though it is fractionally warmer in late summer. In Ramsbury, the Kennet flows over a bed of gravel, and is naturally shallow and swift. But the main channel also runs through a maze of tributary streams, field drains and weirs, mill pools and leats, and, in the case of the manor, a broad and lordly lake. We villagers do not know our river well. The banks are privately owned. Public access is restricted to bridges and one or two other places where custom allows us in (like the old village 'swimming pool' at the back of the fire station).

In chalk streams, most of the small life of the river clings to the underside of stones, or finds other refuges in the waterweed – our champion ranunculus, which puts forth its gorgeous yellow-centred white blossom in May (its botanical name is the stream water-crowfoot). The most obvious manifestations of river life are the famous 'hatches' of mayflies, those brief but spectacular swarms over the water, light dazzling from the dancing wings. At such times, the trout go manic, snatching the winged insects straying too close to the water, or, more easily, gulping them down as the dying flies subside with open wings onto the surface.

The mayfly is the angler's insect. Anglers invented their colourful names: blue-winged olive, March brown, pale watery, yellow evening dun. Fly-fishers need to know their mayflies because they copy their forms as fishing lures – the angler's flies. They also have their own words for the mayfly's habits. The dull fly newly emerged from the stream is a dun, the mature dancing fly a spinner, and after its brief spin is over, the fly is 'spent'. Each stage has its own equivalent artificial fly: art imitating life.

Not all mayflies fly in May – it's only a name. But May is the best month. It's a long while since I've witnessed a big hatch on the main river, but later on my walk I see a small one in the lee of a plank bridge near the manor. From where I stand, the swarm is less a mass of insects than points of reflected light – day stars – silent and ghostly. Beneath the dancers lies the confetti trail of spent gnats, the funeral procession passing downstream, undisturbed this time by feeding fish. The life of an adult mayfly is hardly a life at all: they emerge, they swarm, they mate, they die, all within hours. No wonder they are called the *Ephemeroptera*, the 'brief-wings'. In the quiet, a woodpecker drums; I hear a distant quarrel of blackbirds, a cawing of rooks, the rush of water from the nearby weir. The moment in the life of these mayflies is over for another year.

Michael: This afternoon I was upstairs writing when the doorbell rang. Jo answered it. A neighbour said: 'It's Franko. He's on his roof. He says to get Mike.'

Jo went out into the road and shouted up to the roofs opposite: 'Franko?'

He appeared. He cried: 'It's a wheatear! It's on the chimney pot! Get Mike! Quick!' It transpired later he had rung me but my mobile was in another room and I didn't hear it.

Jo ran back into the house and called up to me: 'Franko says there's a wheatear on the chimney pot.'

I called back: 'What?'

She shouted: 'FRANKO SAYS THERE'S A WHEATEAR ON THE CHIMNEY POT.'

I galloped downstairs, grabbed my bins and ran into the street, shouting: 'Franko?'

He appeared again and pointed. 'It's on the chimney pot over there. It's hawking flies like a flycatcher.'

I shouted: 'Where?'

'Come round the corner. That's it. Now look up to your right. On the second chimney pot.'

I did as instructed and brought my bins up to my eyes. and Lord blow me down with a feather, there it was. *Oenanthe oenanthe*. A stunning springtime male.

'Look at the plumage,' Franko was shouting, but I didn't need telling – the peach flush on the breast, the blue-grey back, the black-and-white face, but more, I saw the restlessness, the twitchy energy that charms everyone, that captivated me when I first saw wheatears as an eighteen-year-old volunteer warden at Newborough Warren nature reserve on the far tip of Anglesey. No scree, no rocky shore, no sand dunes here to bounce around: instead, our rooftop bird was, as Franko said, giving vent to his vitality by hawking flies like a spotted flycatcher, sallying out and back from his chimney pot, the white arse that gives him his name flashing in the sunlight. A sublime, exhilarating spring-time gift. A small bundle of wildness briefly blessing us with his presence, here in the land of estate agents' boards and loft extensions. I was gobsmacked. I still am.

Friday 24 April

Jeremy: Another flawless blue sky. Well, not quite – I can see the first con trail I've noticed since lockdown. The absence of air traffic has been a real boon, in reducing noise pollution and of course air pollution. The quality of the air in London and other big cities has improved dramatically and we've all seen these extraordinary before-and-after shots of famous landmarks suddenly re-emerging from the toxic gloom, the most striking of which has been the Himalayas in all their crystalline beauty, seen for the first time in thirty years by people in the Punjab a hundred miles away. One can almost sense the whole earth breathing again.

I make for one iconic local landmark to pay my respects. It's a black poplar, perhaps the most charismatic of all British trees. We are very lucky to have one in the village. A genuine black poplar, *Populus nigra* var. *betulifolia*, to give the native race its full botanical style, is one of our rarest and most endangered trees, not to be confused with what Richard Mabey calls its many 'characterless hybrids' and cultivars. Only some 7,000 black poplars are recorded in the UK, of which we have a significant proportion in Suffolk, exactly 480 in fact, many of them aged up to 200 years and there-fore nearing the end of their natural life span. They were once much commoner in this county, particularly in wet meadows and flood plains, and you can spot them in Constable's paintings of the Stour valley around Dedham and East Bergholt, for example in his famous 1821 'Haywain'. Oliver Rackham goes so far as to say that the absence of the black poplar in our countryside now is the most significant difference between modern and medieval landscapes.

A mature black poplar has *character*. And the character is one of rugged grandeur. They can stand up to 100 feet high and have a distinctive silhouette, often with a heavy lean and with massive down-sweeping branches. The trunk and boughs are deeply fissured and embossed with large, knobbly burrs. The bark is so corrugated that it's impossible not to want to touch it and run your hands into and over the rough crevices. Our own local tree is set back from the road and surrounded by some large ashes, so it doesn't quite dominate the landscape as some others I know do, for example those at Fen Ditton in Cambridge and at Icklingham in the Suffolk Brecks. I talk of *knowing* them, and you do feel you can know trees as individuals in a way different from one's more generic relationship with, say, bluebells or swifts, if only because they are stationary and long-lived. This tree was here perhaps a hundred years before I was born and could outlast me by as much again. So I pay my annual respects, satisfy myself that our black poplar has survived another winter's storms and watch it putting out its bunches of tremulous heart-shaped leaves into a new spring.

Michael: On yet one more magnificent morning – this spring they seem to be endless – Jo and I walked into Richmond Park though the Petersham Gate and up along the Petersham Slopes, the name given to the long, steep hillside, an extension of Richmond Hill, that runs for more than a mile along the park's western boundary. This is one of its loveliest corners, a terrain of green grassland filled with colossal ancient oaks – in somewhere like Romania it would be called wood pasture, and there would be livestock grazing under the trees. Here, red deer move in and out of the shade. Green woodpeckers were yaffling and stock doves were giving their *ooo-wa, ooo-wa* calls. When we got to the top, we saw once again, from another angle, how the landscape had been mended by the removal of cars, for the grassland flowed out uninterrupted from the edge of the slope over the oak savannah – no other word for it really – towards Pen Ponds nearly a mile away. In normal times there would be a steady procession of motor vehicles along the road a hundred yards in front of us, and the vista would go no further than that.

We stopped to drink our water near a flowering hawthorn and were at once surrounded by big black flies with their legs hanging down so they looked like aircraft coming in to land. I said to Jo: 'It's the bibio. *Bibio marci*. The St Mark's fly. It's meant to come out on St Mark's day. Would you look up the date of that on your phone?' She did: it was 25 April. 'Then they're a day early,' I said. The flies (also known as hawthorn flies) have a characteristic flight – hover, dip, slide sideways – and once you know them you will never forget them. I first saw them about twenty-five years ago, fishing the River Test at Timsbury in Hampshire with my friend the angling writer Brian Clarke; he pointed them out to me and told me how, although they are terrestrial insects, they are sometimes blown onto the surface of the water in large numbers, getting the trout very excited. Brian told me he was once fishing the River Kennet when there was a fall of St Mark's flies onto the water, 'and every trout in the river came up after them. It was quite extraordinary.' He added: 'When I think of the spring, I actually don't think of the mayfly, I think of the St Mark's fly.'

Saturday 25 April

Jeremy: Bizarre news from America, where Trump is promoting the therapeutic properties of disinfectant – a new way of poisoning the body politic there? Meanwhile in the UK we pass the threshold of 20,000 deaths in hospitals, unimaginable just a few weeks ago. People you meet out walking stop a lot to talk of such things now, from a careful distance. It's striking just how respectful most people are of the government's instructions on this and how quickly we have all adapted to these new norms of behaviour, out of consideration as well as fear. It's a welcome paradox that social distancing has led to greater, not less, social interaction and cohesion.

I head along the river to Little Bradley and check out the paddocks, where three horses are nibbling the scanty grass. The ground is hard and dry, but a couple of birds are trying to break through it. A blackbird is stabbing away, but it looks like hard work, with the worms probably quite deep underground. Meanwhile, in the far corner a green woodpecker is using its much more powerful dagger bill to excavate an ant colony and lick up the inhabitants. Green woodpeckers spend a lot of their time feeding on the ground like this and I like the way they hop energetically round their excavations, sizing up the best line of attack.

Horses attract insects, which in turn attract birds, and there are other visitors to the paddock foraging overground.

Three yellow wagtails are dancing around almost under the feet of the horses to pick off the insects they are disturbing. Yellow wagtails are summer visitors to Britain, but increasingly rare ones now that we have fewer wet pastures and wetlands; these two will be just passing through briefly on their way elsewhere, probably to the Ouse Washes or the Fens. All wagtails are delightfully balletic – the Italian name for our commoner pied wagtail is *la ballerina bianca* – but the slimmer and slighter yellow wagtail outdoes the others. These three are so dainty and light on their feet that they are almost floating, as they do their *sautés* and *jetés* in their sunshine-yellow costumes to snatch at passing flies. But this image is the wrong way round – it's the ballerinas that are imitating the wagtails, not vice versa.

Sunday 26 April

Peter. We seem to have three cuckoos in the valley, the same number as last year; perhaps even the same *birds* as last year. As usual they call from the reeds and the scrub near the river, but despite hearing their calls daily, I haven't yet managed to spot any of them. The cuckoos move about within their territories, which are strung out over four kilometres of river between Axford in the west and Littlecote in the east. The western bird I sometimes hear from my cottage; another I hear singing near the road bridge. Everyone knows them, and we are all, I think, thankful they still visit us.

These are, of course, male cuckoos (one of them is singing as I write this). Only yesterday I heard a female cuckoo calling, *quik-wik-wik-wik-wik*, which the books describe as a 'bubbling chuckle', and David Attenborough as 'bathwater gurgling down the plughole' (he really should see a plumber). It was loud and was meant to be heard. The male cuckoo, lurking somewhere downstream, suddenly stopped singing, and then responded, with what sounded like excitement: *cuck-cuck-cuck-coo!* When next I heard it, the bird had flown far upstream towards the Seven Bridges. Did it overshoot? Did it find locating its partner almost as difficult as I did?

In our cold valley, the arrival of the cuckoo coincided with the opening of the first cuckoo flowers. Various spring flowers are known locally as cuckoo flowers, but only two bear that name officially. One is lady's smock, alias *the* cuckoo flower; the other is ragged robin, whose scientific name, *flos-cuculi*, is of course 'cuckoo flower' in Latin. Their connection with cuckoos is the season. Both are in bloom in April and May, at the time when the cuckoo sings (though – alas – all too often they flower where the cuckoo no longer sings). And they both grow in wet meadows and marsh, which in my corner of the world at least is where the cuckoo also dwells during its short stay with us.

Lady's smock is having a good year. It brightens the meadow with its feisty pale lilac flowers, harmonising nicely with golden-yellow buttercups and white chickweed. Ragged robin, on the other hand, is sparse; I have known years when this plant, named after its frilly red petals, is so common as to form a collective haze, a pinkish mist over parts of the meadow. Perhaps the flood of late winter, when water stood in furrows and dips for weeks on end, has crippled its growth. But like the cuckoo, it will be back, renewed and reinvigorated.

To stand among the cuckoo flowers and hear the eponymous bird calling feels like an immersion in springtime. Stand still and let nature soak into your bones. Feel yourself become grounded in the wild. Silence can be exhilarating. Let's enjoy it while we have it.

Michael: Every day for the last week has been filled with brilliant sunshine, and under cloudless skies this morning I walked the Thames towpath from Richmond to Kew. It has never looked lovelier. The green tunnel of the first half, alongside the wooded drainage channel, the Mini Ha-Ha, was decorated everywhere with white flowers: the portly blossoms of the horse chestnuts, the heady-scented may blossom of the hawthorns, the silky white dead-nettles, the white-tipped towers of the garlic mustard, the frilly lace of the cow parsley, which is now chest-high. Blackcaps were singing all the way along, and orange-tips and small whites were flitting about the lady's smock and the crimson petals of honesty (the flower that produces those circular papery seed pods which children used to call 'moon pennies'). When I got to the edge of the Kew bluebell wood – the towpath runs alongside it – I peered as hard as I could; I could see scattered single flowers, but the great swathes of blue are on the far side, and I resigned myself to the fact that that's the end of it – they will flower unseen this year. When I got back, I sat in the garden with a glass of lemonade. It was so hot it felt like July, not April. But that was no compensation.

Monday 27 April

Peter: Yet another cuckoo flower is lords-and-ladies, our own arum lily. There is a particularly fine crop of them this year, lurking on the shady banks of paths and lanes, and I suddenly realised today how they came by their odd name. In place of anything you could call a flower, this plant has a pointed green hood inside which is an erect object resembling a little poker, called the spadix. And while most of these fairy pokers are purple, a few are yellow. The purple ones I take to be the 'lords', and the yellows the 'ladies' (or maybe the other way round, who knows?). The same colour contrast must be behind its country names of Adam-and-Eve and devils-and-angels. Its alternative name of cuckoo-pint is ruder. Yes, the plant appears at the same time as the cuckoo, but the 'pint' is short for pintle, an old word for the male member. It's the cuckoo's willy!

Later in summer, the hood and pintle die back and are replaced by a cluster of orange berries. I nibbled one once, wondering what it tasted like. Big mistake! The berries are not only mildly poisonous; they contain razor-sharp crystals of oxalate that stick into your tongue. It's like biting a mouthful of pins. I'm prepared to bet that not many people have tried this experiment. Otherwise there would be yet more folk names to add to an already lengthy list. Prick-tongue, maybe, or blister-gob, or the berry's revenge.

Michael: Today it was warm but cloudy. The clear skies have gone now, after six weeks. Has there ever been such a period of weather in England, such uninterrupted high barometric pressure, in March and April? Not that I can remember. When we heard the buzzards mewing overhead (see entry for 24 March), Jo and I were sitting in the garden; we were outside having lunch, in *March*. That was unheard of – we usually have to wait until July. But maybe that's it with the good weather now; perhaps the rest of the spring and the summer will be a washout in traditional English fashion, like that whole series of sodden springs and summers we had from 2007 to 2012, when half the country was annually flooded and you had to go abroad to find the sun. No need to go abroad in the last six weeks, though (not that you could, of course). The sunshine has made everything glow, it has brought the growth on so much that life seems to be about a fortnight ahead of where it normally is, and it has been the most wonderful season so far. In the natural world, that is. In the human world, the deaths from the virus in Britain surpassed 21,000 today. I keep thinking: what a bizarre and tragic conjunction of events is the spring in the time of coronavirus.

7

Spring Rain: 28 April–6 May

April showers and the petrichor, wild flowers of suburban streets, ubiquitous muntjacs, reed buntings no longer in the reeds, Gerard Manley Hopkins and the month of May, Sedgie and his repertoire, the first speckled wood, secrets of the red campion, an obscure planarian, dryads of all kinds, and a singing whitethroat

Tuesday 28 April

Jeremy: Well, April showers at last, saving the proverbial expression in the nick of time. How strange that it feels like a relief, but everything is strange this spring. We read that wildlife is moving into niches temporarily abandoned by humans in lockdown – buzzards on Hampstead Heath, deer in Morningside Road, Edinburgh, and a greylag goose nesting in a flower-bed at York station – which only goes to confirm the insight of the Roman poet Horace, 'You can drive nature out with a pitchfork but she'll soon be back.' I imagine the only urban wildlife species suffering are the scavengers like pigeons, gulls and crows that depend on discarded human rubbish. A recent photo of St Mark's Square in Venice revealed neither pigeons nor people.

There are few people out in the rain today here, too, nor many birds evident. I head down my usual lane, which is narrowed by the hedges and trees bowing across it under the weight of the water they are supporting. The hawthorns in particular are gravid with blossom, which saturates both you and your senses as you brush past. I'm also gratefully breathing in all the other fragrances that are released by plants and the earth when rain falls after a long dry spell – the petrichor, they call it, that's 'ichor' as in 'the juice of the gods'.

I go on through the copse to the water treatment plant, as the municipal euphemism has it. It's a decidedly unlovely and unfragrant construction, but often a good spot for birds in bad weather because of all the insects attracted by the sludge. Sure enough, a grey wagtail is bobbing and weaving between the revolving arms of the filtering apparatus. Grey wagtails are so named from their slate-grey backs, but they could as easily have been called yellow wagtails if that slot hadn't already been taken, since their most striking feature is their lovely lemon-yellow underparts, brightest of all on the coverts under those extravagantly long and constantly wagging tails. They actually nest somewhere deep in this clanking machinery, so couldn't be closer to their primary food supply.

Overhead, there are small parties of swallows and house martins feasting on the flying insects. The two species are closely related: indeed, the house martin's scientific name *Delichon* is just an anagram of the swallow's Greek name *Chelidon*, which in turn, through a series of linguistic shifts, is the ultimate source of their shared family name 'hirundine'. The house martins are circling in a higher tier of air than the swallows and are easy to pick out by their stubbier outlines, white rumps and chirrupy calls. They arrived here a few days after the swallows and are still taking up their traditional residences under the eaves of our houses, where they become even closer domestic familiars than the barn swallows (to give those their full official name), which do indeed prefer our barns and outhouses as nesting sites. Both examples of a welcome symbiosis with humankind.

It's still raining hard, so I head back home, where the news from scientists is that despite the temporary emissions holiday the world's climate is overheating – fast, and undeniably. If we 'follow the science', as we are urged every evening in the government briefings, we have a pressing need to use the present crisis as a catalyst to prepare for this next and even worse one. It is a rare chance to make some radical new choices.

Wednesday 29 April

Michael: From today, the government brought in a new way of counting deaths from the coronavirus, by adding people who have died in care homes to the deaths in hospitals – so the figure immediately jumped by 3,811, to 26,097. It is clear now that Covid-19 is endemic in nursing homes, and the inhabitants are succumbing. The *Financial Times* estimates the true number of UK deaths so far at 47,000, which would make us second worst in the world, after the US. But what can you do? What can any of us do? Talk about feeling helpless. You can only hope – once that would have been hope and pray – and get on with your life in so far as you can, and for me at the moment that means observing the spring, which of course is going forward regardless. Not even yesterday's rain seems to have been a setback, even though it was drenching. It covered our car in a thick green foam, or so it appeared to my astonishment when I came out of the house this morning, until I realised what had happened. The car was parked in the street directly under a maple tree, and the downpour had brought down thousands, maybe tens of thousands of maple seeds right on top of it, so many that I had to use buckets of water to slosh them off. It could have been worse. In the summer, if we are parked under that tree, the car is sometimes covered in honeydew, which is the sugary secretion from the bottoms of aphids. The aphids love the rich maple sap, but since it is under pressure, when they pierce the veins of the leaves, some of it is forced straight through them and out the other end, and drops down to the ground, or in our case the car roof. It is so monstrously sticky that buckets of water won't suffice. You need the automatic car wash.

It was cloudy but warm, and the rain didn't appear to be returning. The roads around us were covered in blossom knocked down by the deluge, especially from the big Roman candles of the horse chestnuts – there was so much of it that Richmond council dispatched a sweeper van to pick it up – and looking over it all, my eye was caught by what you might call the wild flowers of the suburbs. There are three of them in particular in my part of the world that I am fond of, growing out of cracks and holes, and they are all aliens, brought here from continental Europe. One is yellow corydalis, a cheerful member of the fumitory family; another is creeping bellflower, coloured the faded blue of old Chinese porcelain; and the third is ivy-leaved toadflax, the charming small snapdragon that colonises walls. They were all visible, but today I decided to have a closer look at pavement plants, and saw much else, especially in the grassy verges of our trunk road, the A316. There was a pink five-petalled thing, with long, long seedpods, which turned out to be common storksbill; a small whitish flower with faint purple stripes, which proved to be dwarf mallow; and a trifling yellow bloom, clearly in the pea family, that research showed to be spotted medick. Harder to identify with my rudimentary botanical skills were what I would crudely describe as two different upright dandelions, but I think one was prickly sow-thistle, and the other beaked hawksbeard. All were thriving. Spring is visible in the suburbs as much as in the countryside, but you have to look harder.

Peter: The trouble with writing about mammals is that on a normal walk you seldom see any. A couple of rabbits, maybe, or a grey squirrel (both of which are naturalised rather than native). More often you see what a mammal has left behind. The greasy badger trails from the wood to the river, knots of their coarse hair caught in the barbed wire, or the twisted droppings of a fox. Alternatively, what the cat brought in, or today's squashed sacrifice to the morning commuter run.

The exception is the deer. We have three species in our woods, fallow, roe and muntjac, and we see all three quite often. Roe deer and muntjac are solitary, while the fallow is a herd deer, the does in one pack, the young bucks in another. Muntjac, that diminutive, bottom-heavy Chinese deer, the progeny of escapes from parks and collections, has taken southern England to its heart. It is the one that enters gardens most, in search of flowers to nibble or tender trees to browse. Occasionally I've heard one scream at night, an unearthly noise, loud enough for you to wake and sit up, startled. Perhaps it couldn't find its way out and panicked. All this month a buck has been calling to its does, a husky bark that carries far. I glimpsed the buck in the hay meadow the other day, slinking along close to the fence, a handsome red-brown animal the size of a Labrador, with tiny-but-sharp antlers and curious dark glands beneath its eyes.

We had a closer encounter today while enjoying a socially distanced drink with the neighbours across the fence. A muntjac doe tiptoed into the garden from the stream, belatedly spotted us, and raced across the lawn straight into the garage. A moment later it had dived through the fence and darted across the forecourt before disappearing into a line of alders. Seen from the back, it looked very like a hare, and was almost as fast. Unlike the buck, it was dark greyish and without the stylish adornments. My neighbour Elaine told me she had recorded muntjac in the garden at night with her infrared camera. They are versatile beasts, alert and timid and yet not at all shy of human habitation. And unlike our native deer, they don't have a defined breeding season, known as the rut; they can breed all year round. With few natural enemies, muntjacs are, in every sense, enjoying a free run in Britain.

Thursday 30 April

Jeremy: I'm walking past one of the big rape fields that dominate much of our landscape now and I hear a familiar song coming from the middle of the crop. A familiar song, but in an unfamiliar place. A bird with a jet-black head and a dazzling white collar is intoning a tuneless jingle from the top of a tall stem. It's a reed bunting – a very handsome bird, but a strong candidate for Britain's worst songster. You do still get reed buntings in reed beds, but as our wetlands have contracted in area the species has spread out to drier habitats as well. They ought really to be called 'field buntings' now. Marsh harriers, too, often nest in arable crops these days, while marsh tits have mainly become birds of woodland.

Other birds have also proved adaptable. Sparrowhawks can no longer survive on a diet of house sparrows, which have gone into a steep decline, despite the massive expansion in new houses. Nor could herring gulls still manage on the depleted herring stocks off the east coast; while our so-called 'seagulls' have become city scavengers, and barn owls have become so short of old barns to breed in that they should probably be renamed 'box owls'.

Meanwhile, some birds have declined so much that their names are just a nostalgic memory. We lost the corncrake from the cornfields around here over a hundred years ago, and the corn buntings are on the way out, too. In other cases, it's an expansion not a decline that has rendered an old name misleading. Chaffinches don't just scrabble around for grains in the chaff of a threshing floor any more, nor do linnets survive only on linseed. And the population of wood pigeons has exploded way beyond woodlands into every garden niche they can commandeer.

Some names never made sense to start with. Mute swans are far from silent, and the common gull isn't at all common most of the year in England; while the oystercatcher prefers mussels and cockles. The meanings of other names are buried deep in their origins. 'Pheasant', for example, literally means 'the bird of Phasis', a river near the Black Sea, from where they were introduced into Europe over two thousand years ago.

It all reminds one of Humpty Dumpty's dictum: 'When I use a word, it means just what I choose it to mean.' Something to bear in mind when listening to politicians deploying the new political vocabulary of 'herd immunity', 'self-isolation' and 'social distancing'.

Boris Johnson announced today that we are now 'past the peak and on the downhill slope', and praised the fortitude and discipline of the British people thus far. We are certainly proving at least as adaptable as birds, but what we don't yet know is which of our recent adaptations we ought to make permanent ones. There have been gains as well as losses in this new and simpler way of living.

Friday 1 May

Michael: May Day, and the hot sun has returned. Is it going to continue through this month as it did through last? If so, this would be some spring. But I wish that we celebrated today more than we do. It's a festival for international labour, of course, and I take nothing away from that, but I do wish we had some sort of ceremony linked to nature, some recognition that May is such an exciting month, charged with life, animated, floral. In France on May Day they give each other bunches of lily-of-the-valley, *muguet* – they habitually call it *le joli muguet,* with the adjective. You don't see much of it here, but there is a border full of it in a front garden in our road, and I went and paid my respects to it this morning. And that was it. However, there is one tradition available to us where May is (or was) properly celebrated, and that is Christianity, and the month's association with the Virgin Mary. This is given its due in one of my favourite poems, 'The May Magnificat' of Gerard

Manley Hopkins, the troubled nineteenth-century Jesuit who struggled so hard with the light and dark of his religion. Hopkins describes May as 'This ecstasy all through mothering earth', and it is thrilling to watch him pushing at the norms of Victorian verse and triumphantly succeeding. This is a passage from the middle of the poem; the word 'bugle' is a reference to the blue wild flower of that name:

> Ask of her, the mighty mother:
> Her reply puts this other
> Question: what is Spring? –
> Growth in every thing –
>
> Flesh and fleece, fur and feather,
> Grass and greenworld all together;
> Star-eyed strawberry-breasted
> Throstle above her nested
>
> Cluster of bugle blue eggs thin
> Forms and warms the life within;
> And bird and blossom swell
> In sod or sheath or shell.

Saturday 2 May

Peter. The sedge warbler is late again this year. Back in the nineties, it was usually singing by the third week in April, but recently I haven't heard it until around May Day. For whatever reason, they do not feel the urge to sing right away. The reed warbler is the same, but in its case you do hear the odd *churr* from the marsh, like a cold engine misfiring.

At last I hear one, and then another. Sedgie is back in its usual place, by the fifth bridge and on its favourite song perch, a sallow bush overlooking an old mill leat. They are amazingly faithful to the same tiny patch of ground; even, as in this case, to the precise same bush. I spot it for an instant; then it notices me, stops singing, and hops behind a fluff of catkins. Sedge warblers have serious expressions. We instinctively make a connection between a bird's eye stripe and our own eyebrows, and so see a chiffchaff, say, as perky and cheerful, but the thick cream stripe of a sedge warbler makes it seem solemn, and even a bit cross. I don't suppose the bird's inner emotions are much different from those of a chiffchaff, though in full song, a sedge warbler does give the impression of being simultaneously desperate to impress whilst also being in a tremendous hurry. Out comes a medley of chatter, *churrs*, whistles and squeaks, faster and faster, like on those old record players we could switch from 33 to 78 rpm just for a laugh.

Unlike some birds one could mention – the chaffinch springs to mind – every sedge warbler sings a different song. A more expert birder than me even recognises sedge warbler accents. Partly this is because Sedgie is an excellent mimic. It can do stand-up! Back in 1995, when nightingales still sang in Ramsbury (though not in the square), one of the sedge warblers managed a perfect rendition of phrases from the night bird's gurgling, churring repertory. Back in 2009, there was another expression of warbler talent, with snatches of chaffinch, blackbird and even skylark. And this year, our fifth-bridge songster has got the blackbird's squawk of alarm off to a T. So lightning fast does the bird flicker from one song idea to the next that the human mind is left far behind. I think of one of those Gilbert and Sullivan patter songs, which only the most rubber-mouthed singers can get their tongues around. I leave Sedgie after a full quarter of an hour, still singing lustily, and scarcely without pause, from its concealed perch yards away. I hope its prospective mate was suitably impressed. I certainly was. If I was a warbler, I'd marry it tomorrow.

Sunday 3 May

Michael: Today I saw my first speckled wood of the year, although the species probably started emerging three weeks ago. I have loved this butterfly since the day I first glimpsed it, which I remember precisely: I was eleven years old and wandering through Dibbinsdale, the valley of the small River Dibbin in the Wirral, where I come from; the butterfly was settled in a patch of sunlight in the woodland gloom. I didn't know what it was, but I was very taken with its chocolate-and-cream markings, and I looked it up when I got home. Speckled wood isn't a bad moniker, but if this were the eighteenth century and you could still give names to butterflies, I would call it the dappled shade, which is its preferred habitat. In fact it is the British butterfly that is most shade-tolerant, and can be found even in very dark woodlands (although in terms of coloration, we have a darker butterfly, the ringlet, which comes out in high summer and, when newly emerged, can appear black). The speckled wood is the first of the eleven British species in the brown family to emerge, nearly as early as the orange-tip and the holly blue: another lovely spring signifier.

I caught up with it in Sheen Wood, where I was pleased to see two new additions to the spring flora: herb-robert and herb bennet. They seemed to alternate in clumps along the main path, the first being a cranesbill, an attractive combination of pink and green, and the second, like quite a lot of yellow, vaguely buttercuppy things, belonging to the rose family (and also known as wood avens). Herb bennet has always struck me as a plant whose five-petalled flower is too small for its stem; it looks as if it's had a job emerging and is just about clinging on, and I find myself characterising it with that old-fashioned adjective once patronisingly used to praise courage in others considered inferior: plucky. *What a plucky little chap he is, that herb bennet.* The names of both plants indicate that they were thought to have medicinal properties, and I idly wondered if visiting American botanists would call them erb-robert and erb bennet, since in referring to herbs, Americans drop the h.

Monday 4 May

Peter: As deaths pile up, this locked-down spring rolls remorselessly on. When spring began this year the landscape of the valley was still wintery and wet. But after five weeks of near-continuous sunshine, the spring is now fast advancing into summer. It has happened so fast. The bluebells have blued and gone, and the flowers of early summer are opening – clovers, thistles, cranesbills, hawkbits. In my garden, red campion has become the lead weed, helping itself to the flower bed, having already taken over the small plot where we once tried growing potatoes. I don't mind. The flowers are comely and shocking pink, and they last a long time. And unlike nursery plants, they have biology. They are real flowers, the way nature intended them to be. Peering closely, you spot that there are two different kinds of red campions, one with a bunch of spindly stamens in the middle of the flower, which is male; the other, slightly fatter, and with a tiny inner floret of white threads, is female. Having male and female flowers on separate plants assures outcrossing, and so good genetic health. It helps that campion is popular with bees and butterflies, despite having no scent. It must work well, because red campion is among the commonest flowers of May.

You can't say the same about its close relative, the white campion. I know patches of it here and there, but there seems to be less of it about than even ten years ago. A verge on a nearby lane suggests one reason why. There we get a third kind of campion, a pink one, which is the hybrid between the red and the white; moreover, it is a hybrid that is fully fertile. I suspect that the scarcer white campion is being hybridised out of existence by its more outgoing relative, wherever they come into contact.

We also have a violet-centred campion. This is a flower, red, white or pink, which has been taken over by a fungus called the campion smut. Instead of producing pollen, these infected flowers contain the purple spores of the fungus inside their stamens (the fungus also changes the sex of the female plants to male so it can use every flower). So as I say, campions are intriguing and full of surprises, and I would rather have such things in my garden than sterile roses that no insect cares about, or plants that have had all their natural science bred out of them.

Besides, campion is such a wholesome name. It sounds very English somehow, though in fact it derives from the Old French word for 'open country'. The meaning of its generic name *Silene* (pronounced Sy-*lee*-nee) is obscure, but it might well commemorate the god Silenus, who was noted for being perpetually drunk. Like him, the flowers are red-faced, and they sway in the breeze.

Tuesday 5 May

Peter: The two springs in my brother's garden, just down the road, are flowing fast and clear. One is a small saucer-shaped basin within a few yards of the stream, itself a tributary of the main river, whose flow is governed by a sluice gate at the mill house. The larger one was once used as a watercress bed. Its rear bank is artificially steep. Cold water bubbles from the foot of the hollow, feeding a sluice of clean gravel that runs down to the stream. It forms the middle of a wonderful wild corner, a garden within a garden marked by a trio of mature poplars and an ancient ash tree. Blue tits are nesting in a hawthorn bush, but our owl box, fitted to one of the poplars, has so far attracted no interest.

I fish about in the gravel bed to see what is living in these gin-clear cold springs. Looking down on it, you would think the water to be near lifeless, but remove some of the stones into an enamel dish and life appears, scuttling, wriggling, crawling, or, in the case of the tiny black limpets anchored to the flints, just sitting there. There are caddis cases attached to the stones, a few young stonefly nymphs with their double-pronged tails, and numerous shrimps, named *Gammarus pulex* from their resemblance to *Pulex*, the flea. There are also skeletons of last year's leaves, as black as Florentine lace.

The most characteristic form of life here is a planarian, a flatworm so obscure it doesn't even have a common name. *Crenobia alpina* is dark grey and less than a centimetre long, with tiny 'horns' and two rather doleful-looking eyes.

It normally lives under stones, but in my dish the worms have come into the light, plainly looking for the way out. I love the way they glide along so effortlessly, without the slightest wiggle or twitch, a slow-moving torpedo of primitive matter. They are cold-water beasts, at home only in these springs and in the headwaters of moorland streams. Without deliberately searching for them, no one would suspect their existence. I put the dish back in the stream and let the running water flush them back into their rightful environment. Though virtually brainless, perhaps *Crenobia* is wise. It lives in a niche of supreme irrelevance to our own careening lives, and bothers nobody. Good luck, little flatworm! Stay safe, stay alert. And above all, stay at home.

Wednesday 6 May

Jeremy: I often pause at Little Bradley churchyard, which used to be one of the best places locally to find a favourite but fast-declining summer visitor, the spotted flycatcher. I think of this bird as the *genius loci* here, the unobtrusive, watchful spirit of the place, probably loyal to this site for centuries. The church is a small but ancient Anglo-Saxon one, and the hummocky field to the east is the site of a deserted medieval village. The gravestones afford this species just the right kind of perch from which to mount its short aerial sallies after flying insects, which are often abundant in a well-managed churchyard – that is, an under-managed one. Benign neglect is an important conservation principle. No luck with the flycatcher again today, however. They are late arrivals so there is still a chance, but I fear we've lost him.

I head into the adjoining grove of mature trees, mostly horse chestnuts and beeches, all in full leaf. It's cool and

shady under the dense canopy here, and you feel yourself
in a separate little world, with its own numinous presences.
There's a large fallen beech straddling the narrow path. It
came down two or three years ago in a winter gale and
now hosts a remarkable growth arranged in large and
colourful tiers on the recumbent trunk. It's a bracket fungus
with the forbidding scientific name of *Polyporus squamosus*
('with many pores and scaly') but the more poetic common
name of 'dryad's saddle'. The saddles (aka 'conks') are the
projecting broad caps of the fungus, soft and smooth to
the touch now, though they acquire a leathery feel later in
the season. They are yellowish or pale tan in colour, with
an attractive patterning of darker brown scales (hence the
other common name of 'pheasant's back'). As for the dryads
who might have sat in these saddles, they were tree spirits
in Greek mythology, especially oak nymphs but with respon-
sibilities for the tree portfolio more generally.

These dryads have had to do some heavy etymological
lifting in natural history. Keats addresses his nightingale as
the 'light-winged dryad of the trees'; then there's the *Dryas
octopetala*, the mountain avens, the alpine tundra flower that
also gives its name to the glacial cycle called the Younger
Dryas; there is even a super-class of tree-nymphs, the hama-
dryads, who became so identified with their tree-homes
that they died with and in them; and these have somehow
been memorialised in the names of a snake, a baboon and
an Australian butterfly.

People sometimes recoil from fungi, because of their
associations with decomposition and their other-worldly
appearances, but they play a crucial role in the world's
nutrient cycles and ecology. Aristotle, the first zoologist in
the Western tradition, made this very point in his manifesto

for the study of natural history: 'There is something to be wondered at in all of nature . . . We should pursue our enquiries into every kind of animal without distaste, since each is in its own way natural and beautiful.' These dryads are other, but not alien. We are part of the same web of life.

Michael: Whitethroats are among my favourite springtime birds. The breeding male is one of our few warblers to approach the rich colour patterns of the dazzling wood warblers of America: he has a grey head, contrasting with a white throat, which contrasts again with a pink-flushed breast, and there are terracotta patches on his wings. Whitethroats are first cousins to blackcaps and have a similarly memorable song, though where the blackcap's notes are melodious and fluting, the whitethroat's are scratchy; however, the song is of equivalent or even greater power. I sometimes think a whitethroat singing sounds as though someone has cut a hole in a packet of frozen peas and started pouring them out, a short but unstoppable flood; and the song flight is even more beguiling. It's as if the bird can't help itself, like something from a thirties musical: 'I never wanted to be an insurance salesman anyway. I only ever wanted to . . . SING!' and he launches himself into space. I feel an orchestra should be swelling behind him. It's not just a sound, it's a spectacle.

Today Jo and I had a memorable whitethroat experience. It was made more so by the fact that the coronavirus news was particularly grim: the UK became the first European country to surpass 30,000 deaths. Little over a month ago, such a toll would have seemed incredible. Now it just seems inevitable. It was on our minds as we left the house at eight o'clock on a sublime morning and walked up through Bog Gate, into the park and over to the hawthorn valley. This is not marked on the Ordnance Survey maps, but is a well-defined area next to Conduit Wood of mature hawthorn bushes or even trees, surrounded by scrub, and is one of the places in the park where whitethroats breed. From the very pretty path leading towards it we saw that all the hawthorns were in flower, a great estate of may blossom, and as we moved into it, we heard the song, and eventually saw the bird. He was on the uppermost spray of a hawthorn bush with the white blossoms all around him, his head raised, singing to the cloudless blue sky. The beauty of it was such that I was shaken; Jo too was lost for words. We watched him in silence until he flew off.

8

They're Back!: 7–14 May

The return of the swifts, Denis Summers-Smith, the lost wych elm of Ramsbury, the Beverley Brook, cow parsley and the seasonal parade of umbellifers, the mystery of the scent of lilac, a garden warbler, Grey of Falloden, the munching marsh marigold moth, brimstone caterpillars, and fox fables

Thursday 7 May

Jeremy: I started scanning the skies for swifts from the first of May this year. They don't usually appear here until the second week of the month, but I've been getting more anxious every year as the numbers of returning swifts keep falling. Will there be one year when they just don't come at all? Mike and Peter and I are emailing each other daily: 'Have you seen them yet?'

People don't often look straight up like this, but it can be a revelation, even if you eventually get 'swift neck'. Today I've seen buzzards slowly circling directly over the house at a tremendous height, riding the thermals and recalling those evocative shots in Westerns of turkey vultures (which the drawling cowboys usually refer to as 'them buzzards'). I've also spotted some sparrowhawks and one red kite going over, and a soaring heron got me excited for a moment, thinking it might be a stork. Then, just as I am about to end the afternoon's vigil at about 5.30pm, there they suddenly are, two swifts shearing through the air. One always remembers the famous Ted Hughes poem at this moment, with its exclamation, 'They're back!' and his sense of relief that 'the globe's still working'. Less quoted are the wonderfully vivid images through which Hughes captures the special charisma of the birds as they career round the houses 'on a steep / Controlled scream of skid' like 'Frog-gapers, Speedway goggles, international mobsters . . .' You should read the whole poem.

We have only two or three pairs of swifts left in this village, and even these are threatened, as the building they usually nest in has scaffolding all round it and is under reconstruction. You'll see and hear them more readily in cities, literally screaming overhead as they chase each other over the rooftops, then whirling up into the skies, only to bank and dive again at wing-shuddering speeds.

Swifts are the most aerial of all our birds. They eat, mate and even sleep on the wing, spiralling high into the sky to take the avian equivalent of catnaps. Sometimes pilots of planes (remember them?) report seeing swifts at great heights, in a stratum other birds never reach, where they harvest a heavenly plankton of insects and (remarkably) airborne spiders ballooning on gossamer threads. They store the catch for future consumption in a special pouch at the back of the throat, bound with their saliva into a ball called a bolus. Incredibly, when the swifts that breed in Britain have reared their young and have left their nests (in crevices in our buildings), they don't touch down again until they return the following year. Their whole lives are spent in the air. They therefore don't have, because they don't need, feet that can grip and perch the way swallows can. In fact, if swifts ever land on the ground, they find it very difficult to take off again. Their scientific name is *apus*, meaning 'footless'. But once in the skies, they are in their true element, designed with a perfect aerodynamic shape to cut through the air with minimum resistance. A truly charismatic bird – and quizzers might like to remember that, as far as I know, it's the only British bird whose full name is an adjective: swift by name and by nature.

Swifts were one of Gilbert White's favourite birds. In a long letter to his correspondent Daines Barrington, he lovingly describes their habits and behaviour, whose mysteries he believes he has largely solved – a result, he says, 'of many years exact observation'. He calls them 'amusive' birds, a word that nicely connects White's twin passions, for understanding nature and for delighting in it. This now archaic expression is given two dictionary definitions: (1) deceptive, and (2) interesting, entertaining or amusing.

Michael: I heard last night that Denis Summers-Smith, the world expert on the house sparrow and all the other sparrow species of Europe and Asia, had died on Tuesday, aged ninety-nine. I was very sad. I grew close to Denis while writing about the mysterious disappearance of house sparrows from London (see the entry for 8 April), and came to admire him greatly for his meticulous scientific scholarship; he was one of the most influential amateur ornithologists in Britain of the last fifty years. Denis changed his mind about why sparrows had vanished from the capital. At first he thought it was the lack of insect food for chicks in the nest; he believed the insects were being killed off by a chemical additive in unleaded petrol. But this was never proved, and later he took a different view, though still one to do with vehicle emissions: he thought young sparrows were being directly killed by particulates, microscopic particles of soot from diesel engines.

This was never proved either, but two years ago, after discussing it with him – he was still going strong at ninety-seven – I managed to dig out the figures for the uptake of diesel-engined vehicles in Britain, and they showed a significant surge immediately preceding the beginning of the sparrows' decline in the 1990s. UK diesel registrations doubled between 1985 and 1990, from 64,000 to 128,000, then leapt to 200,000 in 1992, 340,000 in 1993 and 431,000 in 1994. The resultant pollution will have been greatest in towns and cities, and greatest of all in London, where urban air pollution is worst – in other words, harmful diesel particulates in the air in the capital increased substantially just before its sparrow populations began collapsing. This, of course, is only correlation, and correlation is not causation, but the parallel is striking, and Denis felt it was convincing. 'I think it is the smoking gun,' he said.

Denis had been on my mind, because a week ago, I discovered another house sparrow colony, to go with the one I found in early April near my home. This one I stumbled across in an old graveyard tucked away just off the town centre, the Vineyard Passage Burial Ground, which is one of the hidden charms of Richmond. It's now a secluded garden, full of wild flowers and specimen trees, and a noticeboard lists the twenty-nine bird species that have been seen there. One day I caught the unmistakable sparrow *cheep!* from a bush at the far end, but despite waiting nearly half an hour, I couldn't spot the bird. The next day, however, I went back and saw two of them – I think they forage in the burial ground, and are nesting in the gardens of the neighbouring houses. Old urban cemeteries can be wonderful wildlife reservoirs, and David Goode has a terrific chapter on them in *Nature in Towns and Cities*.

Friday 8 May

Peter. It is VE Day, and Union Jacks wave from the houses along the high street. Our closed pub is swathed in bunting. Loitering in the village square, I count at least six swifts screaming over, in two parties of three. They have been here for about a week now. The ideal place to watch them used to be from the bench in front of The Bell, notebook in one hand, pint of Ramsbury Gold in the other. The swifts nest inside the eaves of a gabled house opposite, which in its time has served as a hotel, an office and a school, but is now a private residence – like nearly all the former businesses in the village. The swifts share the house with house martins, which will soon be busy patching up their old nests of mud along the gable walls. They give a lot of pleasure and are one of the defining sights and sounds of the village in summer.

In the middle of the square, indeed in the exact centre of the village, stands a tree. It is a modest-sized oak, little higher than the nearby rooftops. It was removed from its birthplace in Epping Forest over thirty years ago to replace a much grander tree that had stood in the square for centuries. That great and famous tree, which died in 1983, was a wych elm. It dominated the view of the high street, and came to symbolise the village. It also became the emblem of the Ramsbury Building Society, formerly based in the square. It was known simply as The Tree. Our tree.

People have forgotten the deep shade that was cast by our lost elms. There was even a word for it – umbrageous, the shadows under the elm. Beneath the boughs of our tree, which once spanned the whole square, villagers met to pass the time, to gossip, and watch the world go by. Local children would make a den inside its hollow trunk and clamber up to emerge at the top, far above the street. Around it village life went on: the cycle shop, and the basket maker, the tanyard and the butcher's shop, with the abattoir at the back, and children bowling hoops along the cobbles. They say the old tree, long reduced to a shadow of its former glory, died of Dutch elm disease. I think it rather succumbed to the traffic, which had changed from the lumbering wagons of former days to streams of vans, buses and lorries. Even after it was declared dead, some villagers wanted to keep the standing hulk. There was a referendum, in which a narrow majority voted for its removal, on safety grounds. They say the old trunk parted from its roots with a sigh. Little bits of the Ramsbury tree were eagerly gathered for picture frames and other knick-knacks. Such is the mystic power of a tree. It was one of us, in a way the greatest of us, and its passing was mourned like that of a dear old friend.

Saturday 9 May

Michael: On a day of endless sunshine, I hiked to the Beverley Brook on the far side of Richmond Park: my hunger for springtime rivers had got the better of me. That might sound a strange statement, seeing as I have the Thames almost on my doorstep, but the Thames is a grandiose tidal river – what the French call a *fleuve* – whereas, as a river obsessive, I longed to look at something small-scale that still possesses charm – what the French call a *rivière*; a useful linguistic distinction that simply doesn't exist in English.

The Beverley Brook is more than a brook; it's a river proper, albeit a small one, nine miles long, flowing from the London suburb of Worcester Park to the Thames at Barnes. It runs through Wimbledon Common and then through Richmond Park's eastern side, where it's an attractive clear stream with a gravelly bottom, flowing between pollarded willows. On the banks today there were masses of white garlic mustard interspersed with spikes of yellow rocket. I was hoping to see a kingfisher – long stretches have been fenced off to encourage them to breed – but I was out of luck. However, there were wildlife compensations. A glitzy grey wagtail flew up from the water and began hawking flies on the path right in front of me, and then I saw what I sometimes think is the most beautiful British insect, a banded demoiselle – a metallic-blue-bodied damselfly with translucent wings bearing broad stripes that sometimes seem black and sometimes purple. Takes your breath away. I saw no fish, and was disappointed, until I got back to the footbridge by the Roehampton Gate, and there in a deep pool under an overhanging willow were shadowy shapes keeping station in the current and rising to sip in small insects from the surface. I thought for a second they were brown trout, but I put the bins on them and saw the lack of an adipose fin, and the silver bodies with dark tails, and I realised they were dace: a shoal of them, graceful in every flickering movement. Dace grace.

I sat to drink my water in an oak grove halfway down the walk, and yet again I was forcefully struck by what the absence of motor vehicles was doing to the historic landscape – it was mending it, stitching it back together. I looked from the riverbank across the grassland to Spanker's Hill Wood on its rise in the distance, and I felt I could have been in Dorset. Normally there would have been a stream of vehicles a hundred yards in front of me, and there my view would have come to a dead end.

Sunday 10 May

Peter. The verges of the lane, which only a month ago were spangled with celandine and sunbursts of dandelion, have turned white. White with a foam of cow parsley, interlaced with white stitchwort and equally white deadnettle. Behind, the hedge too has turned white, with the clotted-cream sprays of flowering hawthorn. Like the bluebell wood, these verges are the quintessence of the English spring, but in this case you can follow them for mile after mile, on foot, on bike or from the comfort of your car.

Cow parsley is such a common flower, frothing our lanes in May-time, that you might have expected it to have settled deeply into the public consciousness, with, say, a well-known poem or two, and a celebratory *Times* editorial once a year. But it hasn't. Cow parsley isn't a memorable name (the 'cow' indicates that it is fit only for cows – parsley for animals). Its alternative name of Queen Anne's lace seems to be of fairly recent coinage, and certainly doesn't date back to the reign of Queen Anne. A third name, seldom used, is mother-die, which is unsettling as well as baffling. My own mother used to call it 'kecks', but it shares that name with hogweed and other lookalike wayside flowers. I once used cow parsley in flower arrangements for my brother's wedding, and very pretty it looked. But it was thrown out on the grounds that the pollen would turn the wedding into a sneeze-fest.

I suspect the main reason why cow parsley is unsung is that it is an umbellifer, a large group of plants all with rather similar umbrella-shaped flowers. They have the reputation of being difficult to identify. And yet this is the family that gave us carrots, parsnips and celery, all of which have wild counterparts in the British flora. Their tasty leaves and seeds have also given us parsley, coriander, dill and fennel, not to mention cake decorations made from the candied stems of angelica. Strictly speaking, the umbellifers are in fact among the easier wild flowers to recognise and name. Unlike buttercups or dandelions, there are no really difficult species, nor do they tease us by continually hybridising, as do dog-roses or willows. Once you understand how a plant is put together, ID is simple.

The trick is to look beyond the similar flowers to the very dissimilar leaves, and also to the slips of greenery beneath the flower heads known as bracts. Both come in all shapes and sizes, as do the ripe seeds, a motley array of burrs, capsules and mini bottles. Many species also have distinctive smells. You can whiff wild celery from ten yards away, and the water parsnip growing in the ditch outside offers up a sweet scent of that vegetable when you snap its hollow stem. Another tip is to remember the season. Umbellifers flower at different times. The seasonal parade begins with cow parsley, but in the latter half of May, it is replaced by chervil, easily recognised by its hairy spotted stems and flat greyish-green leaves. Soon after, dominance is claimed by ground elder, with its broad leaves and crowded white heads, and hogweed, that coarse, stout umbellifer whose hollow dead stems remain standing well into autumn (unless you snap them to play sword fights with the kids). Lastly, in July, comes hedge parsley, a smaller, daintier plant with burred seeds.

In normal spring weather, cow parsley is a curiously sterile plant. Insects seem drawn to it only on hot days, when the plant makes a special effort and puts forth a sour, musty scent. Then, quite suddenly, it buzzes into life.

Michael: This evening Boris Johnson addressed us all to signal the first partial end to the lockdown, after seven weeks. We were told to go back to work, those of us who can't do our jobs from home, and we can exercise more than once a day – as much as we like, in fact. We are also now officially allowed to sunbathe. And thank the Lord for that. In April I downloaded a tweet from a woman called Natalie Steed, which said: 'Working on my allotment today (as per the benevolent blessing of Michael Gove) I was approached by 2 police officers who had climbed over the fence (into private property) because a "concerned member of the public" had emailed to alert them to "possible sunbathing".' The government now has a new slogan: *Stay Alert, Control the Virus, Save Lives*, with *Stay Alert* replacing *Stay Home*. But Scotland, Wales and Northern Ireland are sticking with *Stay Home*. Is it really safe to start easing the restrictions? The deaths are up to more than 32,000 and still rising strongly, as far as I can see.

Earlier, for my final single period of exercise, I went on a lilac walk, which is something you can't really do in the springtime countryside, but is perfectly possible in the suburbs. The lilacs are flowering early and splendidly this year, and over a circular course of about a mile, through half a dozen roads, I counted fourteen bushes blooming in front gardens, mainly shading from sky blue to purple, with a few versions of white, off-white and ivory. One was primrose yellow, though my favourite was a bush with panicles of a thundering dark crimson, the colour of red wine. But it wasn't the colours I was interested in so much as the scent, that heady floral fragrance. I smelt every one I could, and tried in vain to work out what it was reminding me of. It's something in my childhood, I know that. I have known it for years; the lilac scent is telling me of some circumstance in my young life, in the Wirral more than half a century ago, but I cannot work out what. Is it a person? A place? A happening? Something bad? Something good? I do not know. I cannot uncover the memory. When I smell the scent, I feel I'm on the edge of it, it's just around the corner, but I never get there. I didn't this evening. I don't suppose now I ever will.

Monday 11 May

Jeremy: Boris Johnson addressed the nation yesterday, announcing that *Stay Home* is now to be replaced by *Stay Alert*, a good motto for naturalists too. I've walked up the hill from Temple End Road to the old airfield, at the edge of my range. On an impulse I turn off towards some woodland I haven't explored for ages. I suddenly stiffen, on full alert, hearing a faint but familiar song in the distance. Is it . . .? Could it be . . .? I walk rapidly to the area from which it seems to be coming, and confirm that it is indeed a garden warbler, singing from dense cover. Earlier (11 April), I sadly reflected that I was unlikely to hear one this year, since I knew of none within walking distance, so this is a happy discovery. The garden warbler is uncommon in these parts now and is certainly not a garden bird. Its song is sometimes confused with the blackcap's, but whereas the latter is a clear fluting, like a short but beautifully enunciated declarative statement, the garden warbler's song is richer, and more complex and sustained, like a lengthy melodic rumination. Garden warblers are also rather harder to get a clear sight of, and even when you do glimpse one through the foliage, they are notoriously nondescript, distinguished, as the guidebooks like to say, by having no distinguishing features.

In 1927, Viscount Grey of Falloden published a book called *The Charm of Birds*, which was a great best-seller in its day. Copies can still be found in second-hand bookshops, but it's a classic now more admired than read. It's a book about the charm in particular of bird *songs*, and Grey makes some nice comparisons of his own between blackcap and garden warbler, suggesting that 'a garden warbler's song seems always on the point of achievement, to which only the blackcap attains'. His book is set in the familiar form of a nature diary, and he has some typically modest remarks to make about the justification for publishing such ventures:

> It is not entirely to exchange information that lovers of birds converse together on this subject. An artist will paint the commonest object in order to bring out some aspect that has particularly struck him. So with watchers of birds, some are attracted by one aspect of a well-known species and some by another. Thus even those of us who have nothing new to tell, may have something that is fresh to say.

Grey is best known, however, as Sir Edward Grey, the long-serving British foreign secretary (1905–16) in the troubled times just before the First World War, when he made the famous remark, 'The lamps are going out all over Europe.' This now has a new resonance, though perhaps more particularly this time in the UK, where well over 30,000 lives have been extinguished in just a few weeks.

Tuesday 12 May

Peter: A month ago, the meadow opposite was bright with dandelions. By now, most of them have turned into clocks, those globes of fuzzy seeds you can blow off the stalk to tell the time (though the hour does depend on how hard you blow). The dandelions have been replaced by buttercups, but the effect is the same: 'Buttercup and kingcup bright as brass / But gentle, nourishing the meadow grass', wrote Edward Thomas. In fact it looks like being a wonderful spring for buttercups. Already the meadow is polka-dotted with their glossy golden-yellow flowers. The buttercup – there are three common species, but never mind – is a generous flower. Though scentless, it provides sips of nectar contained in little pockets at the base of each petal. And it offers bountiful pollen, too, arranged in a mass of stamens surrounding the ovary at the base of the cup.

Buttercups are pollinated by insects, especially small bees. These perform the necessary service of carrying away yellow dust-like pollen on their hairy bodies that with luck will brush off on another plant, onto the sticky pad that leads down to the ovary. But being, as I say, generous flowers, buttercups produce far more nutritious, protein-rich pollen than they need. Bees cannot eat pollen straight from the flower, since they lack jaws to crunch it up. Instead they collect it in baskets attached to their legs, mix the pollen with regurgitated nectar back at the hive, and so turn it into honey. Like bees, butterflies and moths cannot munch pollen either; it is useless to them. But there is an exception to that rule, and today I spot it. In fact it would be hard *not* to spot the pollen-muncher, because there are swarms of them jostling inside each golden cup.

This is a tiny moth called *Micropterix*; specifically *Micropterix calthella*, or the marsh marigold moth (its Latin name means 'tiny wing of the marsh marigold', though they are just as happy chewing buttercups). *Micropterix* is a munching moth. Unlike other moths, it has a functional set of jaws (mandibles), which give a curiously bird-like shape to its little ginger head. It is the most primitive of all moths, close to the ancestral, long-extinct being that gave rise to the hundreds of thousands of species of moths and butterflies across the world. Indeed, were it not for its coloured wings, you would hardly suspect it of being a moth at all.

As a reluctant flier, *Micropterix* is easy to spot. Its wings, held at a steep angle like a pitched roof, are iridescent, like shot silk, and when fresh they flash from golden-green to bronze to black as the sun strikes them. There they sit inside the buttercup, or on the similarly yellow heads of pond sedges, in their locked-down golden world, eating or mating, or maybe just idling around doing nothing in particular. It seems that the full life cycle of *Micropterix* is still unknown, despite its being, in terms of numbers, perhaps the most numerous moth of all. Perhaps there is more to them than meets the eye, though I doubt it.

Watching the marsh marigold moth reminds me of another bug with an even more sequestrated life. The fly called *Chiastochaeta* spends its entire life hidden inside the heads of the globeflower, a golden ball of a blossom known in Scotland as the locken gowan – the locked-up flower. *Chiastochaeta* is nothing much to look at; it resembles a small dark housefly with a noticeably large head. You find it by gently opening the globeflower petals, and there, as often as not, will be several of these little flies, busily supping nectar and laying their eggs among the clusters of stamens – from where the tiny emergent maggots will burrow into the developing seeds. As far as anyone knows, their entire lives are passed within the golden ball. Perhaps they have no awareness of any world beyond it. There they are, in their locked-down lives, reduced to what Boris calls 'the essentials'. You have to wonder: did the fly, at some moment in its past, suffer a pandemic?

Wednesday 13 May

Jeremy: I'm walking on a footpath by a small mixed wood and am lured in by a speckled wood butterfly that is dancing along the edge of a ride. As I approach, it joins another that has been basking on some brambles in a patch of sunlight, and together they spiral up towards the canopy. I'm following their flight when, from the corner of my eye, I sense a movement on the track ahead. I tense. It's one of the gamekeepers advancing purposefully towards me. I prepare myself for our customary exchange. He stiffly reminds me that I am on private property. I evince polite surprise and agree to rejoin the public footpath without delay. It's a complicit arrangement. I know he is doing his job and I accept his right to evict me. He knows I mean no harm and accepts my habitual recidivism. Official business completed, I turn to go away; he relaxes and in a quite different tone of voice asks, 'Found anything interesting?' We enjoy the butterflies together a while and then go our separate ways.

Michael: We have brimstone caterpillars! Jo discovered them and gave a whoop of delight, then took a video of them on her phone and put it on the family WhatsApp group. It was a thrill to see them munching the leaves of the alder buckthorn, on all three of the plants we put in last year – the two in the back garden and the one in the front. The female butterflies found them all to deposit their eggs – amazing how they are able to do it. Already growing fat, the caterpillars are precisely the green of the buckthorn leaves they are eating, and when they rest motionless along the leaf's mid rib, they are virtually invisible. They will pupate later this month and hatch out in July, God willing, to become the longest-lived of any adult British butterfly, because they will fly throughout the summer into the early autumn, and then hibernate behind an ivy leaf or something similar. The warming sun will wake them, and they will become the flashing beauties of next spring, and after living nearly a year, they will mate and the whole cycle of reproduction will begin again. Long may they choose our garden as their nursery.

Thursday 14 May

Jeremy: I surprised a fox today as I walked on the ridge. Actually, more accurate to say that we surprised each other. The fox was trotting along the bottom of a dry ditch towards me, while I was concentrating on a newly flowering bramble in the hedge. We were only a few yards apart when we suddenly saw each other. He – I think it was a dog fox from the brush and the build – paused, alert but quite composed, and appraised me. He then turned, without haste, and retraced his steps. The last I saw of him was when he leapt lightly out of the ditch and cut through the hedge to the other side. He made a strong physical impression – of agility, poise, vigour and menace, leaving me also with a glowing retinal after-image of that rich red fur. Red for danger.

Foxes are common round here, but I don't often have such a close personal encounter. We had met each other's gaze and there was an exchange at some level. Well might he interrogate my intentions, of course. Aristotle defined man as 'the political animal', but foxes too have long been political animals in this village. The Thurlow Hunt was established in the eighteenth century and remains very active, now operating within the rules sanctioned by the 2004 Hunting Act. The estates are managed with sporting as well as farming interests in mind. Quite a few local people are employed in these activities and more participate in them. I don't, for strongly held and felt reasons, but I'm aware of an irony in my position. We wouldn't have all the well-maintained copses and coverts that support the biodiversity I care about here without this tradition. Moreover, most of the estate workers have a knowledgeable interest in wildlife and a genuine concern for conservation through their daily physical engagement with the landscape. They tend to scorn what they see as urban sentimentality about the realities of animal life and death that are ritualised in the traditional hunt.

But there are other ironies within the gaming interests themselves. I see a pheasant stalking arrogantly into a nearby covert in all its gorgeous Aztec finery. This is another political animal. More than forty million of this introduced species are released into the British countryside every year simply to be shot for sport. But to make that possible they have to be protected from their other enemies – notably the fox. The poor old gamekeeper has to ensure a plentiful supply of foxes to be chased, and at the same time pump up the numbers of pheasants to be shot. A dilemma worthy of an Aesop fable, surely: 'The Fox and the Pheasant'? There are no Aesop fables about pheasants, however, because there were none in Greece then, and this Asian species has accreted very little folklore in the other European countries to which they were subsequently introduced. The Romans brought them to Britain, and although pheasants dominate our countryside as no other bird does, they still retain an exotic, alien status.

The fox, on the other hand, features in Aesop more than any other animal – in twenty-eight of his *Fables* to be precise, always characterised as a cunning opportunist, a clever trickster and a survivor. And this reputation survived and was embellished in the rich medieval tradition of tales about Reynard the Fox. In the twentieth century, the fox went on to prove its adaptability and resourcefulness by becoming a successful urban animal, living off discarded human scraps and refuse in city gardens and parks, a great snapper-up of unconsidered trifles. Most people are therefore now more likely to encounter them in the town than the country. Still red for danger, though the dangers are different there.

9

Mid-May's Eldest Child: 15–23 May

A landscape rewilded, birds heard versus birds seen, the seductive scent of the musk rose, yellow flag irises, the small heath butterfly, dying ash trees, village names, an encounter with a grass snake, fairy rings, the Duchess of Burgundy, the two smells of elder, and George Eliot's imagination

Friday 15 May

Michael: The planes are starting to come back into Heathrow. At the start of the lockdown two months ago, there was nothing; this morning I stood in Richmond Park and watched a steady stream of low-flying airliners on their final approach to the airport, not one every ninety seconds as at normal peak periods, but certainly one every five minutes. I was trying to watch skylarks on the grassland just south of Bog Gate and I ended up watching a Virgin 787, a KLM 737, an Air China 777 and a British Airways Airbus A320. (I was a boyhood plane spotter and the habit dies hard.) At one moment I had a skylark in its song flight and the BA Airbus in the binoculars at the same moment.

The Heathrow-bound planes do not actually overfly the park, but they're pretty close – their flight path is about 700 metres to the north of the park boundary – and since they are at less than 2,000 feet, they are very audible, so their absence has certainly added to the lockdown tranquillity. But it is the absence of motor vehicles that has made the real, phenomenal difference, and before I left the house this morning, I had an email from a friend that finally led me to understand what it meant.

Isabella (Issy) Tree, with her husband Charlie Burrell, runs the Knepp Estate in Sussex, the centre for two decades of Britain's major rewilding experiment – the former farmland has been left to 'go back to nature', and the results in terms of wildlife have been extraordinary. Knepp is now the best site in Britain for purple emperor butterflies, and one of the best for nightingales and the rapidly declining turtle dove. Issy was writing to tell me about their latest coup – white storks have bred at Knepp this year, for the first time in Britain since a pair nested on the top of St Giles' Cathedral in Edinburgh in 1416. It's the essence of the new rewilding idea in nature conservation: let's do more than hold on to what we have – let's restore what we have lost.

I was thinking about it this morning walking all over Richmond Park, for everywhere I looked, I could see uninterrupted, sweeping vistas across grassland to woodland, some stretching away for a mile or more. Before the lockdown, every one of these panoramas would have been bisected by a line of traffic, but without motor vehicles, the whole historic landscape felt reunited, knitted back together as an organic whole the way it originally was, and I realised what the coronavirus lockdown had done: even if only temporarily, Richmond Park had been rewilded.

Jeremy: The national mood is changing and people are picking the locks of lockdown. The government is increasingly thinking about economic recovery and wants to see us returning to work. They have today promulgated a new guideline based on the R number (reproduction rate of the virus), which is intended to link their policies with an objective scientific measurement. Politicians and commentators will no doubt be making knowing references to this R number in the weeks to come; but there are others (including some scientists) who fear this relaxation of the rules may be premature. Facts are never neutral and always require interpretation, anyway. Death rates may be declining, but more than 400 new deaths were reported yesterday and some groups are still at great risk. It's a difficult balancing act. The government can sense the disciplines of lockdown fraying and has its own reasons for wanting to restore 'normality'.

But does that have to be the old normality in every respect? I shall really miss the wonderful silences we've enjoyed. The noise levels from traffic are already rising. I can hear cars rushing by now, muffling my ears; and there's a motorcyclist accelerating up the hill with a long, fruity fart, surely revelling in his effect on the soundscape, like someone defacing a virgin-white wall with graffiti. It isn't just the volume of noise but the kind of noise. The sounds and silences of the natural world have a wonderful healing power, partly through their associations or, more literally, *resonances*. I can't pretend that a swift's scream or a rook's cawing is euphonious, but they immediately conjure up for me little worlds of activity and significance, just as surely as a skylark's and a blackbird's song do.

Because of this prolonged sunny spell, we have in any case reached the point of late spring (prematurely, in terms of the calendar), where the density of the greenery is such that birds now reveal themselves much more to the ears than the eyes. They are singing and calling from deep cover, where they are often quite invisible; and even when they are technically 'in view', you very often hear them before you see them. Sound travels round and through visual obstacles like bushes, crops and trees; it approaches us from all sides and all angles; it reaches us at all times of day and in all light conditions; and the signals it carries are just as clear as those from visual messages. Birds themselves rely largely on sound to communicate with one another over life's essentials (sex, territory, food, mutual protection and so on), so we need to listen in to understand them.

We can do a simple test by walking up the Temple End Road half a mile. I'll jot down the results.

Heard but not seen: robin, wren, dunnock, song thrush, pheasant, stock dove, coal tit, goldcrest, nuthatch, skylark, treecreeper, great spotted woodpecker, chiffchaff, blackcap, lesser whitethroat

Heard first and then seen: blue tit, long-tailed tit, yellow-hammer, common whitethroat, chaffinch, goldfinch, greenfinch, blackbird, house martin, collared dove, wood-pigeon

Seen but not heard: buzzard, swallow

Seen first then heard: jackdaw, starling

It is a very unscientific test, of course, but to adapt a parliamentary expression, I think the Ears have it over the Eyes.

It's now nearly sixty years since Rachel Carson published her book *Silent Spring*, which can be credited with launching the modern environmental movement by exposing the effect that pesticides and pollution were having on the natural world, and in particular on birds. It was a brilliant choice of title, recalling the lines by John Keats from 'La Belle Dame Sans Merci': 'The sedge is wither'd from the lake, / And no birds sing', and it owed much of its force to the value people place on birdsong and spring, and on birdsong *in* spring, as a defining aspect of the season. The current pestilence has also demonstrated its importance, but through the contrary and positive effect of highlighting birdsong, not suppressing it.

Saturday 16 May

Peter. As I write, the front of my cottage, and that of my neighbour's too, is swathed in pink blossom. It's a climbing rose, lipstick red in bud, candy pink in flower, faintly scented, and it lasts about a week. One spends far longer pruning the growth and sweeping up the fallen petals than in admiring its brief climacteric.

Further down the lane, however, at Howe Mill, there is a different climbing rose, with small white flowers in bunches, that has scrambled over a willow tree. For a moment in late May, it looks as though the willow itself has freakishly burst into blossom. On warm, still evenings, the scent seems to lie thickly in the air, balmy, silky, spicy sweet.

These are the emanations of the musk rose, *Rosa moschata*. The plant has been cultivated for its unique scent for centuries. It is the musk rose of Shakespeare, adorning the perfumed bower of Titania in *A Midsummer Night's Dream*, and also the 'soft incense' that hangs on the boughs in Keats's 'Ode to a Nightingale'. They say you should plant the rose on the west side of your garden, where the embalming scent will waft over you on the warm, moist winds of midsummer.

In both the play and Keats's deathless Ode, the musk rose is companioned by eglantine, an old name for *Rosa rubiginosa*, the wild sweet briar (eglantine comes from the Old French *aiglantin*, meaning, well, 'sweet briar'). It's a bushy rose with deep pink flowers with a white centre. It too is scented, and not just the flowers but also the leaves. On the latter, the perfume, which smells of sweet apples, is contained in reddish glands of oil that smother the undersides. In mentioning eglantine, Shakespeare may have had a double meaning in mind. This rose is sweet, but it is also prickly. Titania is in for a thoroughly humiliating time once the ass-headed weaver, Bottom, joins her in her bower.

But it was the musk rose, not the eglantine, that seduced Keats; as the poet sits in the dark, listening to the nightingale and smelling, rather than seeing, the flowers around him, its heavy scent is a promise of summer:

> And mid-May's eldest child,
> The coming musk-rose, full of dewy wine
> The murmurous haunt of flies on summer eves.

Keats's famous lines seem to capture the instant when spring turns into summer; or, more specifically, when we experience spring and summer both at once. We have arrived at that moment now. Summer is calling early this year.

Michael: The yellow flag irises are nearly at their peak in our garden pond, and I have been trying to work out why they appeal to me so much. I think it's partly because they're big: dramatic and unignorable, with stems that at their tallest are nearly the same height as me, and flowers sitting on top of them that are appropriately . . . large. Yes, but I think I would use some other word to get their particular appeal across, such as *strapping*. Or maybe *hefty*.

And then their appearance is simple: they are just a great blodge of bright yellow. It's not a subtle beauty, though they do have elegant, lily-like lines – they are thought to be the origin of the heraldic symbol, the fleur-de-lis – rather, it's the fact that there's a lot of it, it's the luxury version, it's an extra helping. But it's a real beauty none-theless. I sometimes think they're the aquatic equivalents of foxgloves, another alluring big plant with large, simply coloured flowers (dark pink in this case) that comes out at about the same time, the end of May, beginning of June.

Most of all, though, I think the appeal to me this year is in what the yellow flags represent, which is wetlands, and in particular rivers, in late spring or early summer, especially the chalk streams of southern England, which, locked down as we are, are now wholly inaccessible. They are the loveliest rivers in the world, and I see the yellow flags above the gin-clear water, with maybe the cuckoo calling, and the dimpling trout, and every now and then a swirl as a fish takes a mayfly. The beauty is heart-stopping. And I see all that ten yards from the kitchen window.

Sunday 17 May

Jeremy: I like to vary my daily walks to keep an eye on all the fast-moving changes in the different places I visit, rather as I'm spending more time than usual in the evenings emailing and phoning friends to hear how they are doing. Time to check out one of my favourites again, the long grassy track I call the ridge walk, a public footpath leading from Great Thurlow to Great Wratting. When I reach it, I discover to my surprise that it has just been mown. Must have been the local council, but why would they do that now? The grass hasn't grown much in recent weeks anyway, and they've beheaded a lot of flowers that were just pushing up – speedwell, forget-me-not, trefoil and vetch – disturbing or destroying who knows what else in the process. Surely they must have better things to spend their money on in the current health crisis? I suppose it's because the path has the official designation of the Suffolk Way, which runs all the way from here to Shotley on the coast, and regulations prescribe a seasonal close shave this week. Well, I've been scrupulously observing lockdown and my beard has grown from New Testament to Old Testament levels of luxuriance and is now heading for the full Methuselah. Couldn't we allow the flowers a similar freedom? Maybe I should write to my MP, who happens to be the health secretary, Matt Hancock . . .

There's still some sparse longer grass either side of the shorn track, though, and I investigate that. Point made, because a couple of small heath butterflies immediately get up and fly on a few yards – more of a flit than a glide, completely disappearing again. These are tiny butterflies, not much bigger than your thumbnail, and are not uncommon but are quite inconspicuous, particularly because of their habit of closing their wings when feeding or at rest. The folded wing has a circular black spot on the forewing with a tiny white pupil, which you can sometimes pick up from a few yards away, but the underside is otherwise a well camouflaged combination of browns, greys and whites. When it flies you get just a flash of the richer yellow-brown coloration – orange-ochre? – on the upper side as it dances away again, but you're lucky ever to get a steady view of it. The small heath is one of the family of 'browns', and has none of the showy glamour of a peacock, a red admiral or a swallowtail. Charisma can be overrated, though, just as rarity can. Rather like the small birds that get dismissed as 'little brown jobs', the small heath has its own subtler attractions once you've learned to distinguish it from its cousins and come to know its ways. Familiarity breeds affection, not disdain. The small heath's specific name suggests at any rate that it has its circle of loyal admirers:, *pamphilus* 'loved by all'.

Peter. I am staring anxiously at our ash trees. It is only now that one can see which ones are dead or dying, and which are just a bit slow in coming into leaf. Ash dieback is a fatal disease caused by a fungus that has wiped out ash trees and whole ash woods across Europe: the tree's own pandemic. The disease was first noticed in Britain in 2012 on planted saplings received from tree nurseries in the Netherlands, and has since spread all over Britain from Kent to the Highlands. I can see dying ash trees from my window, some boughs struggling to survive with bunches of leaves at the tips, and some that have already succumbed. The trees can take several years to die. There is no cure. You watch their slow death helplessly and angrily. Eight years ago, I wondered how a sick ash tree would appear – for ash was always a supremely bountiful tree, bursting with good health, with those affirmatory upwardly pointing twigs. Now we may soon wonder what a healthy ash tree was like.

It is part of the price we pay for planting trees. The late Oliver Rackham, who knew our wild trees better than anyone alive, noted that planting trees to reduce global warming is a bit like telling us to drink more water to keep rising sea levels down. It won't work. I once calculated that you could plant our parish – and Ramsbury is a large parish, twenty-five miles round – with trees from end to end, and they would not even mop up the emissions from our cars. There may be many good reasons to plant trees, but tackling carbon is not one of them. And in the meantime, since many of our planted trees are imported from foreign nurseries, they bring their contagious diseases with them. Does that sound familiar? Can we still learn from nature?

I'm told that rooks used to prefer elm twigs to any other kind of twig to build their high nests, but now that the elms have gone, their next favourite is the ash. Apparently ash twigs are the right shape and bind together well. What will they do when there are no more ash trees? If I were a rook, I think I'd emigrate.

Monday 18 May

Jeremy: The media are now full of features on 'nature experiences' to delight the senses and console the spirit in these troubled times. I keep meeting local people on my walks, too, who are making their own discoveries and are eager to share their pleasure in them. A retired estate worker at Great Wratting always hails me from his garden as I go by to exchange news. He's just tipped me off about a plantation by the river where he heard a cuckoo one morning recently, a bird I'd abandoned hope of hearing this year. He also told me something of the wood's history – it's a plantation of willows, originally planted commercially to produce cricket bats. These must be white willows, whose variety *Salix alba caerulea* was identified in Suffolk in the 1780s; they flourish in wet, boggy soils and produce just the right kind of light, resilient wood you need for bats. He imparts the further local knowledge that a bag of bats from this plantation was presented some years ago to the present owner of Great Thurlow Hall, a cricket enthusiast. Ah, the smack of leather on willow – this May would have been perfect for cricket in any other year . . .

There are clues everywhere about our deeper landscape history. A decade ago I edited a volume about life and work in the Thurlows consisting wholly of contributions from villagers, and I realised then how many natural features here are memorialised in local names: willows for a start, in Willow Hall, and other trees in The Limes, Hollyberry, The Hawthorns and The Firs; flowers are represented in Lavender, May, Larkspur, Honeysuckle, Myrtle and Rose Cottages; birds in Blackbird Cottage, Kingfisher House and the Cock Inn; and mammals in Fox Cottage and Molehill House.

The same applies to the names of Suffolk villages them-selves, which can also tell a story. Trees are prominent features, of course, and were often important in the rural economy, as suggested in names such as Campsey Ash, Elmswell, Oakley, Thornham, Walsham le Willows and, less obviously, Bergholt (birch copse) and Copdock (pollarded oak). Animals crop up too, as in Foxearth, Hargrave (hares), Brockley (Brock, the badger), Wangford Warren (rabbits), Hartest (deer) and Martley (a more surprising one – martens, which were once found in East Anglia). Birds figure in Hawkedon, Falkenham (falcons), Ousden (owls), Elvedon (possibly swans) and Cransford (cranes, common in the wetlands here in the middle ages). There are even fish lurking in Fornham (trout, from the Anglo-Saxon) and amphibians in Frostendon (frog valley); and there is at least one village named after an insect – Knettishall, which literally means 'gnat's nook'.

Most of these old names will have evolved from general custom and practice rather than being decided on at any particular time. They have a history and life of their own, like the places they denote. They may now seem quaint or curious, but they are not wholly artificial, and they remind us how the natural and human worlds were once more fully connected. By contrast, in a fast-growing new town near here, there's a bird-themed estate, whose attractions the planners sought to enhance with such zoologically improbable names as Sandpiper, Tern, Osprey, Gannet and Rosefinch Closes. Gannet! The nearest breeding colony is probably at Bempton Cliffs in Yorkshire. Rosefinch!! Jeepers, I last saw one of those in Estonia. Why not make some space to plant native trees and bushes in these new estates, see what wildlife arrives, as it will, and start a new tradition? Brimstone, Blackbird and Bumblebee Closes? Maybe even Waxwing Way? Names matter.

Tuesday 19 May

Michael: Walking across Lawn Field, a wide area of rough pasture at the centre of Richmond Park, on a hot, hot day, I nearly trod on a grass snake. I was taken aback. It was big, more than three feet long, and a luscious, glowing dark green, and I tried to keep up with it, but it was slithering faster than I could walk and disappeared into the rushes.

I stood there thinking about it. I realised I was delighted to have seen it at such close quarters and been in its company; I felt the sort of animated fascination young children feel at seeing a new and exotic animal. And yet that went against what I was supposed to feel, our inherent fear of snakes and spiders, which is meant to be thousands of generations old and a major evolutionary aid to survival during the aeons in which we walked unshod. I confess I do have an instinctive fear of spiders – nothing I can do about that – but I am not so sure about snakes. I once saw a black mamba, Africa's deadliest serpent, which had been run over on a road in Namibia; even dead, it sent a chill down my spine. Yet spotting the grass snake in Richmond Park left me thrilled. Perhaps it was the fact that I knew it was non-venomous; or perhaps we may have more than one set of feelings inside us about snakes, an idea powerfully explored by D. H. Lawrence in his gripping poem about the one that came to the water trough in the garden of his house in Sicily 'On the day of Sicilian July, with Etna smoking.' Lawrence see-saws between wanting to kill the beast out of fear, and a sense of privilege that it has blessed him with his presence; if you wish to discover which wins out, read the full poem. But certainly, seeing my grass snake today, I remembered Lawrence's lines:

> But must I confess how I liked him,
> How glad I was he had come like a guest in quiet,
>   to drink
> at my water-trough
> And depart peaceful, pacified, and thankless,
> Into the burning bowels of this earth?

Peter. Dark, sinister roundels have appeared on the big lawn next door. Two of them are about the size of a paddling pool, but the biggest is a full six metres across. They look too neatly circular to be natural, more like an archaeological feature; maybe the remains of round huts buried beneath the grass. Around the edge of each circle, the grass is short, brown and dead. Bordering the dead grass on both sides are narrow dark rims where the grass has turned a dusky shade of blue-green.

In pre-scientific times, such circles were believed to be the dance floors of fairies, but for a long time now we have known that they are in fact caused by a fungus, traditionally known as the fairy ring champignon (*champignon*, literally 'one of the open field', is French for 'mushroom'). No champignons have appeared yet, and none will until autumn, but the fungus is nonetheless growing within the soil, interacting with the grass and expanding outwards in a circle, like mould on jam. The smaller circles are, I would guess, already ten years old (assuming a growth rate of about eight inches per year); the big one must be about as old as the lawn – about forty. I have rarely seen fairy rings so dark and shadowy. They are natural and harmless and interesting, but people are funny about their lawns. I confidently expect to be asked how to get rid of them (you can't, short of starting again). When people hear you are an 'expert' on fungi, that's one thing you get asked. The other is 'Can I eat it?'

I have watched the fungi on this lawn change over the years. When I first came to the village, the lawn was of recent origin, sown on imported topsoil over a raft of rubble and timber. Back then, the fungi that sprouted from the grass after the autumn rain could be spectacular: the lawn briefly became a devil's garden of lawyer's wigs, weeping widows, honey funguses, sticky scalycaps . . . These have vanished now, having consumed all the rotting wood in the soil, but in their place there are colourful waxcaps, orange, yellow, copper and black (though they are all the same multicoloured species). Waxcaps belong to older lawns that have settled and haven't been sterilised by fertiliser. Over the coming years, we may see more and more of these latecomers: pinkgills, earth-tongues, parasols, meadow coral. Perhaps if they pastured a couple of ponies on it, we might even get some mushrooms!

Can you eat it? Yes, you can safely eat the fairy ring champignon, supposing you have identified it correctly. But throw away the stalks. They are tough.

Wednesday 20 May

Peter. Today I met the duke, or, since it was female, perhaps I should say that I met the duchess. She was the Duke of Burgundy and she was a butterfly: a small, prettily marked one that lays pearl-like eggs on cowslips. In Ramsbury this duke has lately become a kind of talisman, like the raven, or the great tree that once shaded our square. Last year, Sue Clarke of the charity Butterfly Conservation came to the village to tell us all about this duke, and to my amazement, the memorial hall was packed. A rare butterfly in our midst was felt to be special. The village felt strangely honoured by it. A week or two later, Sue took some of us out to Spring Hill to look for the butterfly, but it was cool and cloudy. No duke came out to greet us.

I have been visiting the hill at intervals this month, looking hard. Our ducal colony is hard to spot, and usually late; Spring Hill faces north, and a near-constant wind cools the grass. In this warm spring, many other colonies will be nearly over. But I still haven't seen a single one.

It is very warm today, hot enough for patches of road tar to glisten and melt, and the insects are manic. My heart misses a beat as a winged entity shoots up from the grass. Yes, it's about the right size and colour! But no, it's a day-flying moth, a burnet companion. Another motion, and another moth flies up: it is the Mother Shipton, whose wings contain a profile of the legendary witch of that name. I criss-cross the down, eyes on the ground. I see several dingy skippers, the dullest, most moth-like of our butterflies, but one imbued with considerable panache. I watch two of them perform a mad dance for minutes on end, circling round one another aggressively (or amorously? One can't tell), their beating wings a fawn-grey blur.

But still no duke. Ah! There! Once you spot the real thing, there's no doubt. When fresh, as this one is, the duke is fiery orange, with fine brick-like markings, lovely black-and-white chequers around its wings, and pale marks on the underwings that have been compared to a row of hand mirrors. Perhaps that is why its scientific name is *lucina*: it is Latin for 'light', but I suspect there is also a connection with St Lucy, whose symbol is a pair of eyes. The generic name, *Hamearis*, is also appropriate: it means 'appearing in the spring'; *Hamearis lucina*: 'light of the spring'.

The surprise is that this duke is a female, which has brighter, more rounded wings and is much less lively than the male. While the latter darts up to evict any passing butterfly or bee, the female tends to sit tight. I watch this one for minutes on end as it opens and shuts its wings, and then crawls, rather than flies, through the grass stalks. At that exact moment I hear a singing whitethroat, the first I've heard on the hill this year. Nice try, Mr Whitethroat, but I'm not taking my eyes off the duke. This is butterfly ecstasy.

Just one Duke of Burgundy in the whole of a warm, still afternoon! Possibly the butterfly has only just begun to emerge from its chrysalis, or perhaps the males are out visiting hawthorn flowers, where they are hard to spot. Very few ducal colonies are large, and normally you do well to see as many as a dozen in a visit (last year I saw *four*). With such small numbers, you wonder how the colony keeps going, year on year. But it seems that Spring Hill is only one of several local colonies that are in touch with one another. This is what contemporary science calls a metapopulation. Just as Ramsbury has a number of outlying settlements – Newtown (where I live), Knighton, Whittonditch – so too has the Duke. If one colony goes down, another will replenish it.

I return home with my tally of a single butterfly. I have seen it again and I am happy.

And why is it called the Duke of Burgundy? Nobody bothered to tell us, and so nobody knows.

Thursday 21 May

Michael: At least a fortnight earlier than normal, the elder blossom is out along the Thames towpath, flat, round inflorescences of tiny white flowers; from a distance the bushes look as if they are decorated with dinner plates. Elder has a powerful folklore; it was supposed to be the tree on which Judas hanged himself, and could be used to summon the devil, or ward him off – take your pick. It was one of the first plants I ever took notice of, because when I was seven years old, my chums and I had a den hollowed out inside an elder bush on a piece of waste ground. I remember to this day how the branches were curiously soft – pliable and pithy – and even then I realised that elder was different from other trees.

These days, like everyone else, I see it more in culinary terms. Elderflowers have a subtle fragrance that has boosted the sales of summer drinks such as elderflower cordial, elderflower pressé and elderflower champagne. Even more delicious are elderflower fritters. You dip the flowers in batter and fry them for less than a minute in hot oil, and the effect is the most filigree tempura you will ever experience (although the faint taste is helped by a little sugar).

A few years ago I came on my bike to the towpath to gather some flowers for frittering purposes, and ended up taking note of one of elder's more remarkable properties: it has two quite separate smells. For late that afternoon Jo stomped in from work and suddenly cried out in a tone that can only be described as lamentation: 'Oh God. The cat's done a wee in the kitchen. You can smell it.' Somewhere in my brain the thought registered that this lamentation concerned me, and made me spring to my feet before my loving helpmeet discovered the real source of the smell and binned it. For it came from the bag of elderflowers I had tossed onto the kitchen table; not from the flowers themselves, but from the leaves. I had forgotten to take a pair of scissors to snip the flowers off, so I had snapped off twigs with the leaves still attached, and as it was raining, the elder-leaf smell had been masked.

Concentrating in the bag, it had burst forth. It is entirely different from that of the honey-sweet flowers: it is powerfully, pungently sour, with an acrid edge that many people consider distinctly unpleasant. I don't mind it, though. For me, the leaf smell brings back a den, hollowed out and hidden, inhabited by seven-year-olds, snug and secret and sheltered against the world.

Friday 22 May

Peter: Sitting alone on Spring Hill (I'm not sunbathing, Officer, honest), I idly watch the butterflies fluttering over the new grass, and wonder what it must be like to be one. At one level, they seem to live quite pleasant, albeit brief lives. They fly, they feed (mainly on sugar syrup), they mate, they warm up in the sun. But at another level, they are completely alien. What must it be like to smell leaves with your feet, to sense faint aromas in the air with huge bobbly things attached to your head? To see only a close-up world, like magnified newsprint, all shapes and shadows? A butterfly always 'knows' what to do: when a rival comes in sight, when the sun goes in, where to find nectar on a complicated flower. And yet at the same time, it doesn't really 'know' anything. There is no learned behaviour, no thought process; only an instinctive reaction governed by its interior chemistry. I decide that a butterfly's perception of life is unknowable. Who needs sci-fi aliens when you have impossibly strange beings just beyond your back door, and indeed, possibly in the cupboard?

Michael: Spring is approaching its completion now, and I've still only seen the one swallow, and that a bird on passage northwards, glimpsed for but a few seconds (see my entry for 20 April). I think I've missed swallows and their low-level stunt flying as much as anything this year, and I doubt I'll see any more, unless the lockdown is lifted completely and we can travel. But after a heart-in-the-mouth delay, the other two aerobatic insectivores I was waiting for did return. The house martins came back to the old houses in Kew village in May, and I finally caught up with their navy-blue elegance on the 14th. A day later, I saw my first swifts, two arrowheads flashing past the window of the loft, and let out a whoop of delight, shouting 'They're back!', as anyone does who knows the Ted Hughes poem.

But there is another point in the swift calendar just as significant, which comes generally about 10 August – that moment when you glance up in the sky and they're not there. You look and look, but eventually you say to yourself: they've gone, haven't they? Yes, they have. And a melancholy descends on you, for even though officially there's three weeks of the summer left, you know in your heart that it's over.

Saturday 23 May

Jeremy: It's another really hot day, could almost be July. Indeed, I'm feeling the spring has rushed ahead too fast. The dawn chorus isn't quite the crescendo of sound it was in late April, and by the afternoon there isn't much birdsong at all; meanwhile the leaves have lost their delicious fresh-ness and already have something of that dusty look I associate with high summer. I pass through the meadows, where the cows seem to be feeling the heat, too. They've retreated to the far end to chew the cud under the shade of a large horse chestnut. A slight relief because there's a bull running with the herd at present, a big black Aberdeen Angus, and I feel wary when they're grazing close to the footpath.

I pause at the rise, sit down to take in the view and ruminate a bit myself. It's a classic English vista: the meadows with cows in the foreground, bordered by a stream lined with willows and alders on one side and by a thick hedge on the other; beyond these a chequerboard of other fields, some arable, some pasture; and straight ahead in the distance the fields sweeping down to the lawns and the imposing eighteenth-century edifice of Great Thurlow Hall. A scene unchanging in its essentials for years. I think back to other springs and summers and what they have meant to me. There's a wonderful passage in George Eliot's *Mill on the Floss* where she speaks of the power past experiences have in creating the 'mother tongue of our imagination' that we can now draw on. Here it is in full:

> The wood I walk in on this mild May day, with the young yellow-brown foliage of the oaks between me and the blue sky, the white star-flowers and the blue-eyed speedwell and the ground ivy at my feet – what grove of tropic palms, what strange forms or splendid broad-petalled blossoms, could ever thrill such deep and delicate fibres within me as this home scene? These familiar flowers, these well-remembered bird-notes, this sky, with its fitful brightness, these furrowed and grassy fields, each with a sort of personality given to it by the capricious hedgerows – such things as these are the mother tongue of our imagination, the language that is laden with all the subtle inextricable associations the fleeting hours of our childhood left behind

them. Our delight in the sunshine on the deep-bladed grass today might be no more than the faint perception of wearied souls, if it were not for the sunshine and the grass in the far-off years which still live in us, and transform our perception into love.

10

In My End Is My Beginning: 24–31 May

May feeling like summer, a spotted flycatcher after all, village wild flowers, lost turtle doves, goldfinches and nyjer seed, looking for hares, the grace and violence of kestrels, the painful bite of a cleg, the lessons of the spring, bee orchids in the Roman ruins, and the dusk chorus

Sunday 24 May

Michael: The lockdown is coming to an end just as this remarkable spring is coming to an end: they have paralleled each other closely. The Covid-19 infection rate is falling steadily now; today 8,951 people were in hospital with the virus in the UK, down 11 per cent from 10,085 this time last week. This afternoon Boris Johnson gave a press conference signalling further relaxations – although first he made a statement defiantly defending his embattled principal adviser Dominic Cummings, accused of breaking lockdown rules by travelling with his family to the north of England. Then he announced that Step 2 in the easing of restrictions will come a week tomorrow, Monday 1 June, beginning with the limited reopening of schools.

It will have been ten weeks of full lockdown and of springtime. The spring seems to be more or less over, and with the extraordinary unending sunshine that blesses us still, it already feels like summer in the natural world. The ground is very dry, even parched, and the grass is turning brown. On the suburban roadside verges, the wall barley is now riotously overgrown and shaggy – it looks like a man who hasn't had a haircut for a year – and in amongst it are the mauve flowers of mallow, like poppies in a corn-field. The baby conkers are already visible on the horse chestnuts; their leaves have exchanged their early lustre for a dry dullness. Soon the first blisters will appear on them, made by the larvae of the horse chestnut leaf-miner moth, which arrived here from the Balkans fifteen years ago, and now turns the conker trees brown in August rather than in November. On the Thames towpath, the filigree fronds of cow parsley have become skeletons and been replaced by the bulkier stalks of hogweed; while in Richmond Park, the bracken is chest high, though that at least is still irides-cent green. There are young birds everywhere.

Jeremy: Much has changed since we began this project, but the sense I recorded at the outset (21 March) of oscillating between two parallel worlds has persisted, indeed intensified. One of unrelieved horror, the other offering some hope and consolation. The restrictions rightly placed on us in the national crisis have created their own matching compen-sations. I've gladly embraced the discipline of travelling only as far as I can walk and found great freedom in exploring just one familiar area. At least, I thought it was familiar until I really looked. Our patron saint Gilbert White again: 'Men that only undertake one district are much more likely to advance natural knowledge than those that grasp at more than they can possibly be acquainted with.' We have only been advancing our own knowledge not the world's, of course, but the point still applies. And the knowledge has been one of better acquaintance as well as factual acquisition, *connaître* as well as *savoir*, an intimacy based on a more sympathetic understanding of something that was already there all around us, and on a closer connection with it.

This last week of our lockdown spring is a good time to revisit some earlier discoveries and catch up with their stories. I've just been back to that strip of new set-aside created by spoil from some diggings (9 April) and it's looking sensational. There's been a wonderful succession of wild flowers from seeds long buried in the ditch – a brilliant rainbow corridor of vetches, campion, trefoil, clover, black medick, speedwell, buttercup, thistle, dandelion, mustard, mallow, ox-eye daisy and knapweed; many of them officially 'arable weeds', I imagine, but they are all flowers to the bees and butterflies I see swarming over them. It's just buzzing and brimming with life – an accidental nature reserve, if only for one spring.

I also walk up to the grassy track whose close shave I was lamenting (17 May). Well, here's a surprise. Sometime in the last week, a most striking flower has emerged right in the centre of the path, just escaping the grim (municipal) reaper by a close shave of the other kind. It has a shortish straight stalk with a rosette of leaves at the base and two more clasping the stem higher up like a sheath, while the flower on top is a gorgeous confection of sculpted blooms, looking for all the world like a bee. Yes, a bee orchid. More exotic in appearance than actually rare, but quite unexpected here today. They can occasionally shoot up like this one year, only to disappear again the next, and I feel we have been as privileged as the flower was lucky.

The next pleasure is an anticipated one, and none the worse for that. I go on further down the track, where both whitethroats (common and lesser) are singing from the hedge, as are some yellowhammers, whose early silence had got me worried (3 April). One of these canary-yellow buntings is sitting up nicely on a stray hawthorn spray and giving us the full stutter-and-wheeze performance. Bunting – what a nice old word; etymology uncertain, but probably denoting 'plump'. And there's another kind of bunting singing from the rape fields, a reed bunting – yes, we've clocked your incongruous name before (30 April).

I'm clearly on a roll today and I feel I must pay one last visit to Little Bradley churchyard, which I've been monitoring so closely since early May, hoping for the return of its tutelary guardian, the spotted flycatcher (6 May). I'd almost given up hope, but I'm thrilled to find it very close nearby, fly-catching from some overhead wires, back for one more year at least. Thrilled and deeply satisfied. Such a plain, unobtrusive bird, no song to speak of, but a triumph of character over charisma.

Monday 25 May

Peter: It no longer looks like May. The may blossom – the hawthorn – has melted, and the hedgerows are now patched with the flowering shrubs of midsummer: elderflower, privet, with its heavy scent, and, since we are a chalk district, plenty of dogwood (which smells disgusting) and guelder rose. Where it is spared the mower, the grass has grown tall: foxtail, cock's-foot, oat-grass, upright brome. Here and there are mini meadows of ox-eye daisy. We seem to have a great affection for this plant, to judge by the frequency with which it is sown in 'wild' flower seed mixes. Maybe it's because it is like a child's drawing of a flower, white petals radiating from a yellow centre. In our church-yard it has been carefully preserved by the mower, presenting ovals and rectangles of tall daisy surrounded by short grass.

The 'escaped' flowers of the village help to define the streets in spring and summer, even when they are barely noticed. A flint wall of my neighbour's is powder blue with trailing bellflower. It needs no prompting; it appears year on year, revelling in this warm, dry weather. The square has sprouted some street poppies. Their dusty, flame-coloured flowers burst from their buds in the morning on the sunny side of the street, but in the shade of the after-noon, the petals fall, turning bright red as they shrivel. In what only seems like hours, they are replaced by seed cups the shape of champagne glasses on long, straggling stalks. This is not the familiar scarlet common poppy but the lesser-known long-headed poppy. The common poppy colours our corn, but the long-headed poppy brightens our streets! Maybe if it had a better name, it would be better loved.

Along Oxford Street, a little plant with small yellow flowers and weird maroon-coloured clover-like leaves peeps from cracks wherever the pavement joins the brickwork of a wall or house. This is creeping wood sorrel, a plant that has become so cosmopolitan no one can remember where it originally came from. Seemingly delicate, it is in fact tolerant of drips and droughts alike, quietly spreading along the street by means of strawberry-like runners. A gardening website notes that 'it's impossible to get rid of, so we may as well enjoy it'. I think we do, at least to the extent that nobody has yet dealt it a squirt of weedkiller.

One of my favourite village plants is the Duke of Argyll's teaplant. Its weak stems, with their narrow grey-green leaves, arch from a tod of ivy on the corner of Union Street. Every summer it is cut back with the ivy, and every spring it defiantly sets forth again, opening its mauve flowers, followed, if the hedge pruner is kind, by orange berries the shape of a jelly bean. It is named after a famous duke (his portrait is on the Scottish five-pound note), who planted this and other exotic plants in his estate at Whitton Park, near Kew. You really can make tea out of its dried 'goji berries'. Not very nice tea, perhaps, but full of healthy vitamins and carotenoids, and so very good for you.

If all of Ramsbury's streets, houses and landmarks were removed, so long as you knew your street flowers you could still work out where you stood, often within a few yards. No one planned or planted them. They are truly wild, in the sense that they are independent from mankind, from our aspirations and eagerness to tame the landscape. They have found a little bit of the village environment in which to survive, if not flourish, and there they sit, brightening our streets in late spring. We may hardly notice them, in the way you don't really notice wallpaper, but to me at least they make a pleasant antidote to the close-shaved banks and verges, and the fussy little gardens of daffodils planted around the village signs and benches. Nature will out, given just the ghost of a chance.

Jeremy: We've all been watching and listening to (and sometimes touching, tasting and smelling) the wildlife in our patches, with greater attention than ever before. It's sometimes more difficult to notice absences than presences, but there's one absentee that has brooded over every spring here for some years now, engendering an almost palpable sense of loss. That's the turtle dove. I've just checked my old notebooks. We had turtle doves singing and breeding in the village every year up to 2008, usually returning about 5 May; and then it was as if the line went dead. It's been the same all over the country. A few pairs hang on at traditional sites, but the overall national decline has been steep, pervasive and seemingly irreversible. We've lost some 95 per cent of our breeding pairs in the last fifty years. In the brutal scientific verdict, the bird is now 'functionally extinct' in the UK. And the silence is deafening.

The turtle dove was the soundtrack of summer. Its rich purring song seemed to rise from some deep well of common memory into present consciousness. This was the song that heralded the season of growth and warmth, 'when the voice of the turtle is heard in the land'. The song is so powerfully evocative that it defeats direct description and we reach for synaesthetic metaphors: it is the smell of hayfields; the feel of a deep, restorative massage; the slow after-taste of an English beer; the sound, as Mark Cocker once happily put it, of ripening corn.

But why does it actually matter, if you don't feel any of these things? What is lost if one more failing species plays out its Darwinian story and leaves the stage, as thousands have done in the past? What is the human interest at stake here? Not the sort of interest to be measured by narrow economic criteria, to be sure; nor just dismissed as the sentimental reaction to inevitable secular change. The difference now is that we are ourselves the major agents of such changes.

Perhaps there is an analogy with human languages. Some 1,500 species of birds are on the official 'red list' of endangered species worldwide (from a total of about 10,000).

There are some 6,000 living languages in the world today, but similarly, 1,500 of them are spoken by fewer than 1,000 speakers, and on current trends over half the total may have disappeared by the year 2100. With each passing we risk losing a rich and irreplaceable cultural heritage – a unique, subtle and complex way of relating to the world and to other people. Languages too are living organisms, containing within themselves all the memories, understandings, distinctions and associations that encode a culture. When we lose a language, we lose with it a little world and a whole realm of meaning.

Birds like the turtle dove, cuckoo, tree sparrow and corn bunting, all once part of my landscape here but now gone, are also unique carriers of meanings: through their associations with seasons, places and times; through their interactions with other species; through their voices and behaviour; and so through their roles in our own lives. Each one we lose drains the landscape of some part of its significance. We turn out to be the only species with the power to make a dead planet or to create meanings in a live one.

Tuesday 26 May

Michael: The goldfinches came to the garden bird feeder today, with their young. Like so much else this spring, the breeding of birds seems to be coming to a climax earlier than usual: normally I would have expected the goldfinch family in June. We already have a family of young blackbirds following their parents around our borders, picking up tips on how to grab worms, and they're entertaining, but it's the goldfinches that instantly catch the eye, with their bright crimson faces (missing on the juveniles), black-and-white heads and yellow-and-black wings. They are an ornament to any garden, and they represent the great bird-feeder success story of the last twenty-five years: a small black grain, nyjer seed. Originating in Ethiopia, this is the wonder of all bird seeds, and goldfinches cannot resist it, because its nutrient content is very high and it is easy for them to husk; they pick it from the feeder and snip the husk off all in one movement, then swallow the kernels. Put nyjer seed out, and goldfinches will come. Greenfinches love it too, but they have been hit hard by a disease called trichomoniasis and their population has fallen in recent years by nearly two thirds; we haven't had a greenfinch in the garden for a decade.

Goldfinches are a blessedly familiar sight from our suburban kitchen window these days – a generation ago you had to go into the countryside to find them – and their long, buzzing twitter has become a familiar sound from the surrounding rooftops. I think they're the most beautiful bird we get in the garden, but perhaps not the most exciting. In cold winters we get siskins and redpolls, and we always have redwings eating the cotoneaster berries in January; once, in a snowstorm, we had half a dozen fieldfares, a spectacular sight. But the most exciting of all arrived in November 2017, and we learned of it when Franko the birder rang our doorbell and said, 'D'you know what you've got in your back garden?' We did not; it turned out to be a charming warbler, a lesser whitethroat. But not *just* a lesser whitethroat – it was the Siberian subspecies, *blythi*, which should have been spending the winter in somewhere like Iran. Amazing or what? Franko wanted to put details of it online, pointing out that it could be seen from the alley at the back of our house, so that local birders could twitch it, and we agreed. For the rest of the winter, especially at the weekends, we would come down in the morning and from the kitchen window see half a dozen figures in cagoules, fifteen yards away, peering intently through our trellis fence with binoculars. The bird stayed all winter, more or less based in the garden – I last saw it on 12 April 2018. I hope it made the journey home successfully, from south-west London to Siberia.

Wednesday 27 May

Peter: This evening I drive up to Rudge Farm in the rolling chalk country south of our valley. I haven't seen a single hare this year. I sometimes used to spot a few on the walk to Littlecote, especially in the spring, when they famously go manic ('mad'), racing about and braving up to one another (though most of the 'boxing' seems to be done by female hares, testing the vigour of a potential mate). As so often, one wonders whether it is the decline of hares or the decline of one's eyesight that is the problem.

But there are plenty of hares still at Rudge Farm. The farmer, Peter Wilson greets me by a barn over which half a dozen swallows are swooping (so that is where they have gone this year!). He tells me he often sees up to half a dozen hares from his tractor, or from the platform of the high seat in the corner of the big field. At night-time, using an infrared camera, he has seen more. The animals seem healthy. He says he's seen buzzards taking half-grown hares. Previously the only animal they had to worry about, apart from man, was the fox.

He points me to a broad grass strip following the field north to a line of planted poplars. Look out for the barn owl, he says. A pair of owls is actually nesting in his barn, though admittedly in an owl box. With more regret he shows me his new-planted chicory, which has tempted the hares to come close to the farm. The plants are still rooted, but most have been carefully nibbled, in hare-sized bites. The chicory was intended for the birds: its seeds are plentiful and nutritious, and they last a long time. Finches love it. Or they would have.

I finally spot an actual hare at the far side of the field, dark against the stubble. It sees me before I see it. It sits up, black-tipped ears erect, wondering if I'm a danger. Deciding I'm not, it ambles on, bottom-heavy, with an easy, unhurried lope, and then sits up again. I'm still there. Finally it canters off to the far corner, still in no great hurry, and disappears into the hedge. There is an old country word, 'hare-gate', meaning a hole in the hedge just big enough for a hare. I expect it knows all the hare-gates round here.

That is the end of my brief encounter with a hare. It is peaceful up here, in the cool of the evening. Shadows lengthen across the field. The leaves of the poplars rustle in the light air. A late skylark sings from on high. And nearing the farm, the swallows are still active, chittering their song of summer.

Thursday 28 May

Michael: In Richmond Park, the kestrels are now feeding their young. Their nest is in a hole in the sawn-off top of a dead oak tree, about forty feet up. It is quite close to a path, but the birds seem surprisingly at ease with the proximity of humans; both the male and the female bring back prey – voles, lizards, even small birds (it tends to be the male who catches the birds) – with people watching them from quite close by. With the binoculars you can see the young in the nest cavity, staring back at you.

For Jo and me, these lovely falcons have been one of the highlights of our lockdown walks this spring. There seem to be several pairs of them in the park, not least because the landscape is ideal: extensive woodland to nest in, and great swathes of grassland over which to hunt. It is acid grassland, with a different flora from the chalk grassland I know better on the Wessex Downs, and I am gradually growing familiar with it, spotting the blue-petalled, white-eyed flowers of germander speedwell, the tangy yellow roundels of mouse-ear hawkweed, the tiny white bushes of hedge bedstraw and the small golden Maltese cross that is tormentil, a plant I have always loved for its name, which sounds like an invention of Tolkien ('Tormentil, son of Badladriel, leader of the elves of Fordorbor'). It also holds a plentiful supply of field voles, the kestrels' principal prey.

In April, Jo and I watched a female kestrel swoop down on a vole not fifty yards from us. It stayed on the ground for perhaps a minute and we wondered what it was doing; having spoken to several people about it, I now think it may have been eating the vole's brains. It then flew right past us with the small bundle of fur in its talons. This fearlessness is one of the birds' great attractions – we have been close to them innumerable times – along with their unfailing grace. When the pair in the dead oak tree leave the nest, they do not fly up, they dive down in a sweeping shallow parabola that is a joy to watch – Gerard Manley Hopkins captured the movement perfectly in his kestrel poem, 'The Windhover': 'Then off, off forth on swing, / As a skate's heel sweeps smooth on a bow-bend . . .'

But the most dramatic of all our sightings this spring was today, right at the season's end. It was late afternoon and we were about to leave the park at Bog Gate when we saw something weird: the largish wing of a bird projecting from a bramble bush about fifteen yards away. What?? We looked closer and saw to our amazement that it was a male kestrel, which had dived right into the brambles to get at a blackbird's next. The female blackbird was going nuts, screaming her alarm call and diving at the kestrel's head. The falcon was unmoved; a few seconds later, he lifted himself majestically out of the bush and its thorns, and flew off with the male blackbird in his claws. Violence and elegance combined: we were awed by the sight.

Friday 29 May

Peter. A horsefly bit me, quite painfully. It had crept up behind me and sank its rending, tearing mouthparts into my calf (earlier on, it was probably biting a different kind of calf in the neighbouring field). It felt like the stab of a needle, but by the time I reached round to swat my assailant, it had already departed. They say you can tell what kind of horsefly it is from the place it strikes. One likes to go for the back of your neck, another prefers the wrists, and a third, the cleg, will bite you anywhere but prefers to sneak up on the soft tissue behind your knee. This one, I decide, was a cleg. A female cleg, for the male fly feeds more innocently on nectar. The female needs her regular blood meals to supply enough protein for her eggs.

There is beauty even in so unprepossessing a bug as a horsefly. They have huge rainbow eyes, with psychedelic patterns. Some of them are also impressively big, in one case nearly as large as a hornet. Yet these really big flies seldom bother us. We are too small for them. They have set their kaleidoscopic eyes on bigger prey than mankind, on four-legged mammals such as horses and cattle. I maintain that anything in nature that makes us feel humble – a roaming pack of bears, for example – is probably good for our souls. To realise that a huge, greedy fly regards us without interest as just another medium-sized mammal is to know true humility. Perhaps, as theologians might say, that is why God gave us the horsefly.

Saturday 30 May

Jeremy: President Trump spends his Memorial Day in the US on the golf course. No bogeys reported, except those imagined in his tweets about Obama, Pelosi, Biden and the Chinese; and he scarcely mentions the fact that Covid deaths in the US are now close to 100,000. Meanwhile, in the UK, Dominic Cummings gives his *apologia* – which turns out to be more a defence of his lockdown flit than an apology for it – in the Downing Street Rose Garden. No doubt his reasons were sincere, but were they good reasons?

It was in another rose garden, in T. S. Eliot's 'Burnt Norton', that a bird invited us to pursue the echoes of meaning there, but warned that 'humankind / Cannot bear very much reality.' We can be forgiven for feeling confused and disoriented by the extreme contrasts in this extraordinary spring: between the record-breaking sunny weather and the looming climate crisis; between our innocent and inspiring experiences of nature and the tragedies in human lives wrought by the pandemic; between the many individual acts of solidarity and kindness and the cynical calculations of political discourse. We seem to have learned so much and so little.

We have also been charting various beginnings and endings, in both the natural and human worlds. Further on in the *Four Quartets*, in 'Little Gidding', Eliot explores the thought that 'to make an end is to make a beginning'. Perhaps that in itself is the lesson. People have been losing themselves and finding themselves in all manner of worthwhile activities as solace in this very dark time: in gardening, music, art, reading, writing, playing, physical exercise and, of course, companionship and love. In our case, also in nature. The seasonal cycle we have been charting is just that, a cycle, in which the end of one season is the start of another, which in turn brings us back to the beginning, but not quite the same as we were before. Hopefully knowing more, caring more, and more deeply grounded and connected with the only world we have.

Sunday 31 May

Peter. I counted fifty-one bee orchids. They are growing among the low flint walls that 1,700 years ago formed a stately Romano-British villa overlooking a courtyard and a bathhouse, whose mosaic floor still survives. The orchids, brown-and-yellow 'bees' on mauve-pink petals, have found a niche in the ruins of lost civilisation, as have a pair of jackdaws, which have built their muddy nest in the roof beams above the mosaic, and the little owl that nests in a box attached to an over-shading oak tree. As I rest my bike, and drink some water, I admire the orchids, but I can't help viewing them with mixed feelings. For one thing, they are routinely cut down before they can set seed. And for another, this year they are flowering a good two weeks earlier than normal. Bee orchids belong to midsummer, not May. And summer butterflies, too, meadow browns and common blues, are on the wing before their time. The buttercups are fading, and newly fledged blue tits are visiting the garden feeder. This incredible spring of 2020 is nearly over. It feels like summer now.

We are getting used to extreme weather. It has been the sunniest, driest May since modern records began (in 1929), following a similarly dry, sunny April. But that run of sunshine was preceded by two of the dullest, wettest months in recent memory. Man-made carbon emissions seem to be putting an end to climate normality. In the near future we will need to learn how to live not only with a nasty disease but also with increasingly unpredictable weather. But all the same, we might concede that these past two months have been a remarkably benign form of abnormality, for the time we were allowed out to enjoy it.

And now lockdown is being relaxed, bit by bit. Today, on this last of our cloudless May days, I cycle past the still-calling cuckoo, past the oaks and beeches in mature leaf and the bramble thickets coming into flower. Knowing that this will be my last nature note, I feel an unexpectedly sharp sense of loss: a realisation that not only has the spring come to an end, but also my explorations of the parish. Ramsbury has been my window on the world during this season of duality, of sunshine and shadow. Nature has been my consolation, as I know it will have been for many others, in town or country. For nature is not confined, as we were. The observation of wildlife, or even the mere awareness of it, takes us outside ourselves, away from the routines of life, the dire headlines and the daily grind. All we need to do is to look and listen. But to do even that we need space, a sense of calm and quiet. Our world has grown too loud. Others have remarked on the silence that suddenly entered our lives after flights were cancelled and the usual road traffic diminished nearly to a halt. Instead we heard the birdsong, the wind in the branches, the buzzing of bees. When will we hear it again, unsullied by noise? Will that be the abiding memory of this Covid spring – the quiet? The simple silence of a locked-down existence was for some of us a rediscovery of the other world lying beyond our daily preoccupations and our bustling lives.

Jeremy: The last day of the season. The weather has held to the end and seems certain to break all records, just one more phenomenon defining this unprecedented spring. There are crowds out today, enjoying the sunshine and anticipating the end of lockdown. It feels as though it is effectively over anyway, with some people going back to work and some schools opening from tomorrow, a Monday. Perhaps the days of the week will start meaning something again soon, having lost their quotidian significance for the last ten weeks. Meanwhile, spring has already anticipated summer in many of the changes we've been observing so closely – the leafing of the trees (oak and ash both out now), the emergence of flowers and butterflies (meadow browns are already on the wing), and the arrival of migrant birds (all done a couple of weeks ago).

I decide to mark the end of our spring by recording a dusk chorus. Most people know about the dawn chorus of birds, that wonderful succession of different voices, swelling into a full concert as the day breaks. The different species join that chorus in a definite and largely invariable sequence, which you can time as they come in one by one. But there is also a dusk chorus, as they bow out in pretty much reverse order. It doesn't have quite the same volume, but it has its own, more poignant and valedictory, quality. It's also harder work to record accurately, since you have to note down everything singing at each timed interval and later work out the last appearance of each species.

It's a fine evening, though there's quite a high wind, which I hope will drop later to help me, and the birds, hear more. I base myself in our garden, occasionally walking up to a hundred yards away down the lane to increase my radius and range. I start my countdown at 7 p.m., with a new check every fifteen minutes to start with – it will be down to every five minutes later, and then every minute towards the end of the performance. There are thirteen species still singing at seven o'clock: wood pigeon, stock dove, collared dove, song thrush, blackbird, robin, dunnock, wren, blackcap, chiffchaff, goldfinch, chaffinch and green-finch. They all keep going until 8 p.m., when the greenfinch drops out; then the goldfinch at 8.15; the chiffchaff and blackcap call it a day at 8.30, and the chaffinch, stock dove and collared dove at 8.45. I think the wren and dunnock are finished then too, but they return for a brief curtain call at 9 p.m.

We're now down to four – the woodpigeon, robin, blackbird and song thrush. The official time of sunset today is 9.10 p.m., but they are all still going strong then. I hear a swift go screaming overhead at 9.15, scoring a trail of sound across the darkening sky. I'm concentrating hard now, checking every five minutes. The first bat flits by at 9.20 – a pipistrelle, I think. Ah, not so much flitting by as criss-crossing just a few feet above me – there must be moths on the wing that I haven't noticed. At 9.25, a big surprise – a small duck flies over from the direction of the river calling, a sharp whistle. I know that call – it's a mandarin. I see them occasionally down the river, escapees from a nearby wildfowl collection; in fact, one came down our chimney the other year, perhaps investigating it as a nest-ingsite (they are hole-nesters in trees). But that's another story.

The moon is out, in its first quarter, when you can see exactly half of it. A tawny owl essays a few quavering notes as the twilight fades. The tension is building now – well, in me, it is. I'm checking every minute to hear who will outlast the others. The wind has mercifully dropped and there's a lovely evening calm, in which all the remaining songsters have a beautiful clarity. All still going at 9.30, and at 9.35; then the blackbird sings his last melodious notes at 9.36 and falls silent. I can't help hoping the dratted wood pigeon is not going to win this. No, he finishes his crooning litany at 9.43. It's down to two now, and it's quite dark. A minute later, at 9.44, the robin brings his sweetly musing song to a gentle conclusion. It's the song thrush who sings out the spring at 9.48 p.m. He'll be singing in the summer at dawn tomorrow.

Coda

Michael McCarthy

Sunday 31 May

At eight o'clock on a pure and perfect morning, Richard
Deverell unlocks the Lion Gate and lets me in to the Royal
Botanic Gardens, Kew. The Director has agreed to talk to
me about the springtime that has passed unseen inside the
gardens, which are reopening tomorrow after 71 days. It
has been the longest closure, he believes, in Kew's 261-year
history.

It is a thrill to be back in such a beloved place, especially
to be in this lush green landscape with virtually nobody
else. Such has been Richard's experience for the last ten
weeks; the director's house backs directly onto the gardens,
and this has been his site of self-isolation. 'There was hardly
anybody else in these 330 acres – it was surreal and slightly
unsettling,' he says. 'And it was very quiet. For the first
time you didn't have the planes coming over.'

I am keen to hear his impressions of the season that I
and thousands of other people could not see, and as we
walk towards the bluebell wood, his description bursts forth.
'Well it's been this extraordinarily beautiful spring – this
glorious weather, lovely light – the plants, the trees, the

flowers I think have never looked better, and a number of the horticulturalists who have worked here for thirty or forty years will say the same,' he says. 'And they've all got different theories why that is – there's the very wet winter, there's the hot, dry summer last year, et cetera. But for whatever reason, it was the most vivid, extraordinary explosion of colour, and this area where we are now, coming into the arboretum, was just wave after wave of colour, with the wild garlic, the bluebells, of course, the yellow alexanders; it was just unbelievable. It was like walking through a sort of impressionist painting really, these great blobs, bursts of colour, everywhere you looked.'

It is evident that the pandemic has coincided with Kew's most magnificent spring ever, and has actually enhanced it by taking out the aircraft noise, which can shatter the peace of a soft spring day in the gardens like nothing else. It is such a day now. Blackcaps are singing sweetly in the morning quiet. Around us, the stalks of the expired bluebells lie flat and disintegrating on the ground, and I try to picture it in my mind, the blue smoke on the woodland floor with the trees rising out of it. Richard briefly makes it real: he takes out his mobile phone and shows me pictures from 18 and 25 April, the two weekends when I had guessed the bluebells would be at their peak; and there it all was, the violet haze, and also the stunning white carpet of the ramsons. On days like those, Kew might have had 15,000 visitors, he says, agonising about the resultant 'massive hole' in the finances of the RBG.

He has thought deeply about the pandemic, and especially its environmental implications, and he agrees that we have been presented with a remarkable chance to rebuild things in a different way. 'I think we've got this extraordinary moment in time,' he says. 'The so-called green recovery – there is an enormous opportunity to do that, around the world, and I hope it happens. But it requires leadership! It requires far-sighted, excellent leadership, and I don't know whether we are going to get that or not.

'I just hope all this has given humanity a little dose of humility. I think as a species we believe we are masters of everything, that everything can be controlled, and shaped to our will – and broadly speaking that is true. But every now and then, whether it's an Icelandic volcano going off, or an earthquake, or now this pandemic, we are reminded that there are forces out there that we can't control, at least not in the immediate term, and our inability to control them has very profound consequences on our lives.'

Later that afternoon, looking back on the whole spring, I think about Richard's words. I'm walking along the Thames towpath, which at Richmond riverside is crowded with people – the lockdown seems to have been forgotten. I carry on through Petersham Meadows and up into Richmond Park, and I wonder, will people take a lesson from the coronavirus pandemic; will we realise that this is indeed an extraordinary chance to rebuild economies in a better way? Can we put things back together in a manner that will ease the terrible pressures on the natural world, from climate change to wildlife destruction? Will we realise we are not the masters of nature that we think we are?

I walk over to the road between Richmond Gate and Roehampton Gate, still free of cars, meaning the ancient landscape is still blessedly reunited – for now – and I find the bench at the highest point in the park, from where you can see the faraway skyscrapers of the City. It is astonishingly clear, no doubt because of the fall in road traffic pollution; the sun is catching the dome of St Paul's, perfectly visible more than ten miles away, and Wordsworth's line about seeing London's buildings from Westminster Bridge comes straight into my mind: 'All bright and glittering in the smokeless air.' And as I sit there, a whitethroat pops out of a bramble bush not ten yards away, and launches into his song flight.

Beauty right in front of me, beauty in the distance – it is a fitting end to the coronavirus spring, the loveliest spring that ever was. I have never looked so closely at nature before, and I think I have learned something worthwhile: that the more you observe it, the more there is to observe, and you realise that the richness of it is infinite. I am only sorry to have learned this at a time when the damage and the hurt being done to human society has been so immense; yet because of that, to go out each day observing has come to seem like a solemn act. In the end, it was almost like an act of faith – faith in the natural world, in its ability to console us, to repair us and to recharge us; most of all, its ability simply to be there, often unrecognised and unacknowledged, but giving life to every one of us, even as human artefacts are crumbling all around.

Index

Note. Scientific names are confined to those discussed in the text.